T0307779

Pr. ⌐ι *Off the Rim*

"Basketball and North Carolina go together like a horse and carriage. Fred Hobson knows because he lived it. If you love basketball, you will love this book."—Bill Bradley

"I've read most of Fred Hobson's books and admired his relaxed and seemingly effortless style, but *Off the Rim* is his best, in my opinion. This is Hobson at the top of his game, using the first-person narrative like an inmate who has sprung his lock and flown free."—John Egerton

"*Off the Rim* is a marvelous basketball memoir, sprightly and entertaining, and it will take a place on the shelf alongside great autobiographies of fandom like Tim Parks's *A Season with Verona* or Nick Hornby's ruefully comic *Fever Pitch*. But Hobson also brings to the task his experience as one of the South's most distinguished literary critics and commentators, and along the way he provides thoughtful and moving ruminations on race, on family, and on coming of age in piedmont North Carolina in the 1950s and '60s. A delightful account not only of what sports mean to us but of *why* they matter."—Michael Griffith

"Fred Hobson has written a lovely, wry account of his lifelong devotion to Tar Heel basketball. He knows that he stands out even among Tar Heel fans for how much Carolina-blue blood he bleeds and how often he bleeds it, and he also knows that readers will find his obsession more amusing than he does. Even if you don't care who wins the Carolina-Duke game—is that possible?—you'll enjoy this book."—John Shelton Reed

Off the Rim

Sports and American Culture Series
Bruce Clayton, Editor

Off the Rim

Basketball and Other
Religions in a Carolina Childhood

Fred Hobson

University of Missouri Press
Columbia and London

Library of Congress Cataloging-in-Publication Data

Hobson, Fred C., 1943–
    Off the rim : basketball and other religions in a Carolina
childhood / Fred Hobson.
        p.   cm. — (Sports and American culture series)
    Summary: "Hobson, a passionate follower of North
Carolina basketball who once played briefly for the Tar Heels,
tells the story of an eternal childhood relived each season.
More than a basketball memoir, his account also depicts a
seldom-viewed South through glimpses of a boyhood in the
Carolina hills"—Provided by publisher.
    ISBN-13: 978-0-8262-1643-4 (pbk. : alk. paper)
    1. University of North Carolina at Chapel Hill—Basketball.
2. North Carolina Tar Heels (Basketball team) 3. Hobson,
Fred C., 1943–   . 4. Yadkin County (N. C.)   I. Title.
II. Series.
GV885.43.U54H63 2006
796.323'6309756565—dc22
                                                        2005032003

Designer: Jennifer Cropp
Typesetter: Crane Composition, Inc.
Printer and binder: Thomson-Shore, Inc.
Typefaces: Cochin and Cocktail

For Jack and Annabel

For Barbara

Contents

Preface

The child is father of the man.

How else can I explain it? Why else should it mean so much? Why else should I approach each college basketball season, particularly that part of it known to much of America as March Madness, with such a mixture of delight and terror, euphoria and dread? Why should a particular game, played with a round ball by twenty-year-olds in short pants often hundreds of miles away, mean so much to me, since I seem to have so little to gain or lose by its outcome? I get no promotion or raise if my team wins, no financial gain, no book contract, no social benefits, no recognition. Still, I confess, to my great shame and discredit, that I experienced deeper joy when North Carolina (there, I've revealed my bias) won each of its national championships than I ever did over any raise or book contract or the successful resolution of any number of international crises. And in the various years — say, most recently, 1995, 1997, 1998, 2000 — when the Tar Heels lost in the Final Four, I suffered more acutely than I have ever suffered because of financial failure or unrequited love.

Several explanations for my condition offer:

1) Arrested development. If it's true of Bobby Knight, could it be true of me? As all time stopped for an earlier generation of southern boys just before two o'clock on that July afternoon in 1863 when Pickett began his charge at Gettysburg, did all time stop, or at least subsequently cease to have the same meaning, for me on that Saturday night in March 1957 when Joe Quigg hit two free throws to beat Kansas and Wilt Chamberlain in triple overtime (in what Frank Deford has called the greatest college basketball game ever played) to win the Heels' first national championship? The image on the blurry television set that I saw as a thirteen-year-old is fixed in my mind. The child is father of the man.

2) Limited fulfillment in my own life. That is, one identifies with a successful group of some sort in order to fill a vacuum in one's own life, just as one identifies with a great leader: Franklin Roosevelt, John Kennedy, Martin Luther King, Bear Bryant. Ah, the easy answer, one for the shrinks, but I plead not guilty. While there have been no transcendent successes, in general things have rolled along pretty well.

3) The opposite of No. 2: The world is *too* much with us. My life is too full, too complex, national problems are too overwhelming—I need an escape. Sport is a safety valve. Also untrue. Sport is an escape *to* tension. "Enjoy the game," they say as they take your ticket at the door. *Enjoy the game?* Impossible.

4) True involvement; or arrested development, part II. I did, it is true, once briefly wear Tar Heel blue. Thus, the moment, also fixed in my mind, at which the child, now

the man-child out of the Carolina hills, overachieved in October walk-on tryouts and thereby won the right to guard Billy Cunningham in practice and, in games, grace the bench of the Tar Babies (for such was the name given the freshman team that, for a while in 1961–1962, was called the nation's best). Was my tenure on the Tar Baby bench too brief? My moments of glory too few? But that would be the shabbiest excuse, the most shameful admission, of all. Arrested development, part I, is preferable.

5) The most complex explanation but perhaps the truest of all: the impression on the part of the viewer (or listener) that he or she can actually control the outcome of a game three hundred — or three thousand — miles away. If you leave the room for five minutes, your team will rally. If you flat-hand the ceiling twice, the other team will choke from three-point range.

And, during the regular season, not only the particular game at hand but the scores of numerous other games drifting in can be controlled through the manner in which you receive them. No game is an island, entire of itself. If, in Lawrence, the Jayhawks lose by fourteen, then the Bruins climb back into the top ten. If, in Lexington, Kentucky stumbles often enough, the Tar Heels — currently number two — will reclaim the all-time lead in games won. Games have consequences. The ripple effect. Robert Penn Warren's theory of history applied to sport: all Wednesday night games in February compose a gigantic web; all are related. If you touch the web, "however lightly, at any point," the vibration reaches "to the remotest perimeter."

I understand all that, but I am still confounded by the

power the game holds over me, and I think I am not alone. In the narrative that follows I speak largely of Tar Heels—and of other things related to growing up (and not quite growing up) in North Carolina—but what I say also holds true of others who find themselves in emotional bondage to Hoosiers and Bulldogs and Ducks, to Wolverines, Gophers, Badgers, and various other species of upper midwestern low-lying ground fauna, to Blue Devils and Blue Demons, Sun Devils and Demon Deacons, to Hawkeyes and Buckeyes, Longhorns and Sooners, Tigers and Wildcats and Lions and Cougars and all other breeds of cat. In the telling I hope I have discovered, among other things, why I care so much. It's because I once cared so much, and it was knowledge carried to the heart.

The child is father of the man.

Off the Rim

1

Walk-On

Old Woollen Gym has long since been eclipsed as the home of basketball at the University of North Carolina — first by Carmichael Auditorium and then by the Dean Smith Center — but on a particular Monday night in mid-October 1961 it was the center of my universe. On the gleaming court, beneath a banner proclaiming the 1956–1957 Tar Heels national champions, tryouts for the 1961–1962 freshman team were about to begin, and to me it was no small matter. Neither was it to a number of onlookers who were anticipating Carolina's finest freshman team in years, and were also there to see a changing of the guard. The previous summer Frank McGuire, the dapper Irishman who had led the Heels to the 1957 championship, had resigned as Tar Heel head coach (under some pressure, because of his freewheeling ways and excessive spending habits) and his low-profile twenty-nine-year-old assistant, Dean Smith, had been promoted to the top spot. This meant Smith was no longer freshman coach, but he was still on hand to see the celebrated recruits — who would all have to play on the freshman team, no matter how good they were, since that was the NCAA rule in those days. Also on hand were Ken Rosemond, new coach of the freshman team, and his assistants, Joe Quigg and Danny Lotz, stalwarts on the '57 championship team.

I probably don't need to say that I was not one of the celebrated recruits the fans had come to see, but I was as curious as anyone else to see them in action—particularly Billy Cunningham, a 6'5" leaper from Brooklyn already becoming known as the Kangaroo Kid, and Jay Neary, a slick guard also from New York. Cunningham and Neary—as well as the homegrown all-state scholarship players, Ray Respass, Bill Brown, and Pud Hassell— didn't have to worry about impressing the coaches. They were already in. But for the ninety walk-ons, more than half from North Carolina but a good number from out of state, particularly the Northeast, the moment was critical. We had four nights, four practices, to show we were better than the rest. Only eight of us would stick on the team.

The tryouts came at a moment of high drama on the Carolina campus. Four days earlier my political hero, President Kennedy, had spoken at University Day in Chapel Hill, warning of perils and challenges ahead and issuing a version of his "Ask Not" challenge. Even more on my mind—and a headline story four days running in the *Raleigh News and Observer*—were the deaths, by cyanide poisoning, of two Carolina students, roommates, found in their beds across the hall from me on the second floor of Cobb Dorm. After a week authorities had still not determined how they died—that is, how the cyanide had gotten into their systems—and rumors, fueled by a couple of other recent mysterious deaths on campus, haunted all of us, especially in Cobb Dorm. When somebody said the cyanide probably came in the form of gas and had been sprayed under their door, we all stuffed towels under our doors. But that didn't help me. I was certain that my roommate, silent and moody, was the murderer, and I would be next. In fact, he was guilty of nothing but being a loner from Syracuse, but that was enough for me, a provincial from the North Carolina hills, to convict him. By the time it was announced—a couple of weeks later—that the deaths had been murder-suicide, I had already moved out of Cobb Dorm to safer quarters.

So basketball tryouts were not only the moment I had waited for all summer and early fall but also a much-needed distraction. I showed up at Woollen Gym in my Converse shoes and white shorts, signed in, shot around for a while on one of the side goals and, after the whistle blew, joined one of six layup lines. Mine happened to be on the main court, and I was one of fifteen or so players headed for the goal under the championship banner. A layup line is what I had hoped for because it would let me do the one thing I could do best—jump. All the coaches had their eyes fixed on center court, ready to give each of the walk-ons, as well as a couple of the scholarship players in my line, a look, when it was my turn to take off from midcourt. I took a pass about the foul line and headed in for the right-handed dunk I had mastered in high school. I planted my left foot, palmed the ball, got good liftoff, and felt confident about it until the ball started to slip out of my right hand. Sweaty fingers dammit. Instinctively, at the top of my jump, I grabbed the ball with both hands and slammed it down.

I had dunked with both hands —something that, till then, I'd never even thought about doing. You have to be able to jump five or six inches higher to dunk with both hands than with one. And, suddenly, I had done it, not really meaning to. As I trotted back to the end of the passing line I heard a few murmurs: a 6'3" white guy in those days was not supposed to be able to dunk at all, let alone two-handed. Was it the adrenalin or the springy wooden floor—or both? I wasn't sure, but I tested it again the next time I was up and again dunked with both hands. The first time I hadn't been absolutely certain, but this time I was sure Coach Smith, as well as Rosemond, Quigg, and Lotz, were looking at me.

After the layup drill came a half-court scrimmage in which I played better than I had ever played before. Five-on-five, and I was guarding Doug Jackson, another walk-on but an all-star forward from eastern North Carolina I'd read a lot about. In twenty minutes I blocked two of his shots, got several rebounds, and went three for three from the floor, hitting twice from what would now be three-point range. Cunningham nodded to me when I walked off the floor. Another couple of players asked where I had played high school ball. The coaches said nothing, but they had seen.

That's the way it went all week. Tuesday through Thursday nights I showed up at Woollen Gym at 7 p.m. and every night the number dwindled as most walk-ons were cut. Each night the layup line—more dunks for me, both one-handed and two — ball-handling drills, defensive drills, rebounding drills, and then a couple of scrimmages. I managed to hide my ball-handling and defensive weaknesses, and the scrimmages, though no longer spectacular, were solid.

But it was the dunks that let me know I had made it. I looked at other players in the layup line, and — amazing as it might seem now — only three others could dunk: Cunningham and Respass and one other walk-on. Given hoop stereotypes and historical realities, a question arises: were all these players white? In 1961 the answer, in the upper South, wasn't automatic: Carolina had been integrated, a little more than tokenly, for several years, and the year after mine a black walk-on did make the freshman team (although it would be five more years before the first black scholarship player, All-American Charlie Scott, was to arrive). And there were a couple of black walk-ons my year too, but no, neither could dunk, and neither made the team. So I was the designated leaper. A 6'8" guy with no hops asked me if I had lifted weights to build up my legs. I had not. In any case, the coaches now called me by name, and they knew where I was from and what I'd done in high school. They hadn't seen me play before — in high school I hadn't been good enough to attract attention at Carolina's level, and my high school team hadn't made the state playoffs in nearby Durham — but now they had evidently done some checking.

When the roster was posted Friday morning, I wasn't even surprised. I knew I wasn't that good but I knew I had *looked* that good, and I was the second walk-on listed.

When I went to botany class later that morning, Cunningham, probably the best freshman in the country (and a future three-time All-American and Hall of Famer), came in and plopped down beside me—the supreme compliment since basketball players hung together and this meant, there being nobody any better around, that I would do. That night, as I went into the dining hall with two or three non-hoop friends, varsity captain Larry Brown (another future Hall of Famer) yelled at me on his way out, "Hey, Hobson, let's go get our stomachs lined." Like Cunningham, Brown was a New Yorker, and I didn't know what the hell he meant. But I yelled back, "Yeah, Larry, let's get our stomachs lined."

It was as good as it got—and as good as it was ever to be.

2

Yadkin

It should have been football. And it probably should have been Duke, not Carolina. Nobody in my family had ever played basketball before, but a lot of people in my mother's family had played football, and all for Duke University or its predecessor Trinity College. In the 1890s my Grandfather Tuttle had played three years for Trinity, and then—in graduate school—another three years for Vanderbilt, there being no NCAA in those days to prohibit such practices. "One of the swiftest halfbacks ever to don Trinity togs," Robert Tuttle was called by one newspaper, "a terror to all Southern colleges."

He had not been the only Tuttle to make a name for himself in the days when teams such as Trinity and Vanderbilt and Sewanee held their own with Georgia and Alabama and Tennessee, when Duke went to the Rose Bowl after hiring away Alabama's famous coach, Wallace Wade. My mother's first cousin, Lee Tuttle—known in the family as Cuddin (i.e., Cousin) Lee—had also starred for Duke in the 1920s but was remembered largely (even in the late twentieth century) for once, in the face of an

oncoming rush, punting backward over his head. Uncle
Bob Tuttle, my mother's brother, had also played football
at Duke but mainly had excelled as a track star, setting a
number of Southern Conference cross country records.
And Cuddin McGruder Tuttle, on his way to becoming
rear admiral, had captained the football team and made
one or two All-American squads at the Naval Academy
in 1931, before surviving Pearl Harbor in 1941 and com-
manding the ship—he later told me—on which young
Paul Bryant, not yet known as the Bear, had served in
World War II. All of these Tuttles fell into the family tradition of what would have been called in the late nineteenth century "muscular Christianity"; as I look at their
football photographs, with leather helmets and no face
masks, I see the innocence and terrible earnestness of an
age still more Victorian than modern.

So it could have been football, and it could have been
Duke, not their arch-rival eight miles away, the University of North Carolina. And in fact it was football for me
at first, but it was never Duke. For patriarchy reigned in
those days: while my mother's family had all gone to
Trinity and Duke, my father had gone to Carolina, and in
my very earliest memories Carolina meant three-time All
American Charlie Choo-Choo Justice, still—more than a
half century later—the best and the most celebrated football player in school history. Before I was seven years old
Carolina had been to three major bowls; in the fifty years
since they have been to none.

Those were truly the glory days of Tar Heel football,
the only glory days, and my earliest awareness of an outside world came in radio broadcasts from Kenan Stadium

as the Tar Heels took on Texas and Tennessee and Notre Dame—and, when I was six, from a trip to Chapel Hill to see Choo-Choo Justice and fellow All American Art Weiner play their last regular-season game, a 21–20 win over Duke. The first newspaper articles I remember reading were about Justice and Weiner, and my first class "papers" in the third and fourth grades were on the history of college football. The glory days could have lasted; they were supposed to last. After a slump in the early 1950s, Carolina hired as head coach an alumnus, Jim Tatum, who had just won a national championship at Maryland, and Tatum was going to take the Heels all the way to the top. "I don't think winning is the most important thing," he said, Lombardi-like, in a newspaper interview. "I think it is the only thing." But Tatum died at age forty-five of Rocky Mountain Spotted Fever after only three years in Chapel Hill, and Carolina's football fortunes died with him—along with my conviction that football was the most important thing in life. But for a random tick bite, Carolina might have been a football school—and Dean Smith a math teacher back in Kansas.

From what I have written you might think that my father was also an athlete and a sports fan. In fact, he wasn't much of either, but he was a loyal Carolina alumnus, and he tuned in football and basketball games with the same calm sense of duty with which he paid his alumni dues. Unlike my mother, who would have been called a city girl in the rural North Carolina of that time, he was a farm boy who had gone to Chapel Hill for an education, not for sports and frivolity, and had come away with a degree in history and a deep commitment to public service. After spending almost a decade as a teacher and then an educational supervisor for the New Deal's Civilian Conservation Corps, he took the job of public school superintendent in his native Yadkin County at the age of thirty-three—a job he would keep until his retirement thirty-three years later. Four years before he came back he had married my mother, and I can't believe she was as enthusiastic about moving to the tiny county-seat town of Yadkinville (population 750) as he was.

The Yadkin County they came to—and where I was born and grew up—is located in North Carolina's northwestern piedmont, in the foothills of the Blue Ridge Mountains. To its east is Winston-Salem, then with its tobacco and textile factories (and the chocolate-like aroma of tobacco filling the downtown air), and to the west is Wilkes County, home of moonshiners, bootleggers, and stock car racers, including rip-roaring Junior Johnson, the "Last American Hero" of Tom Wolfe's famous 1965 *Esquire* piece. Yadkin lacked the drama of Wilkes, but in most other ways it was identical—rural, conservative, independent-minded—and it too had its share of moonshiners, as well as a kind of reflected glory. It was directly on the route between Wilkes County and Winston and thus, on weekends, those bootleggers' cars came through in the middle of the night, their rear ends dragging with their load.

Yadkin was also next door to Surry County, where Andy Griffith had grown up—and on which he was to base his down-home Mayberry and its environs. Yadkin County, just across the Yadkin River, was also Andy Griffith country, friendly, putting on no airs, altogether devoid of class consciousness—unpretentious with a vengeance. Of course, it had never accomplished much on the national, or even the Tar Heel, stage. In politics, literature, the arts, and all else, it would have seemed to the outsider an awe-inspiring blank. It had virtually no industry, and was the only one of North Carolina's one hundred counties never to have had so much as a foot of railroad track. It was relentlessly unprogressive.

Yadkin had, and has, produced few famous sons or daughters, with the possible exception of a couple of athletes—Ernie Shore, who in 1917 pitched an "unofficial" perfect game for the Red Sox (unofficial because he had come on in relief of Babe Ruth—then with the Red Sox—who had gotten himself thrown out of the game after facing one batter; Shore proceeded to retire twenty-six in a row), and Dickie Hemric, who as a Wake Forest basketball player in the early 1950s set Atlantic Coast Conference records for scoring and rebounding that, fifty years later, still stand. Yadkin was also deficient in what some would call high culture, and it was deficient in irony. The town theater owner, who was crippled, was called Crip; the Ford agency owner, who was vastly overweight, was called Chunky. Everyone called them that to their faces—they called *themselves* that—and they didn't seem to mind.

Although this was a southern town, I did not have one of those classic *To Kill a Mockingbird* southern childhoods, filled with racial intrigue and drama—which also meant that I missed out on having one of those classic, though half-forbidden, interracial friendships celebrated by Deep Southerners. As were all North Carolina counties in the foothills and mountains, Yadkin was predominantly white—more than 90 percent—which did not make it any less racist in its attitudes than the rest of the South, just less likely to act on its prejudices. My only close contact with blacks came in the form of Callie Hauser, an intelligent and industrious woman who occasionally helped my mother with housework. Callie sent all her children to college and, if she had lived long enough, would have seen her great-granddaughter featured in the television production of *Roots*.

The county was just as devoid of religious as of racial diversity. Almost everyone was Methodist, Presbyterian, or Baptist, although there were several varieties of the latter—regular (i.e., Southern) Baptist, Primitive Baptist, Premillennial Baptist, and so forth—as well as a few Churches of God and Churches of Christ (which were usually lumped together as "Holiness"). There were also a number of Quakers, who had migrated down from Pennsylvania in the late eighteenth and early nineteenth century, although as they appeared in the mid–twentieth century they were far from the Earlham-Haverford antiwar, pro–civil rights variety of Quaker you would find in the Northeast and parts of the Midwest. In fact, they seemed no different than other rural Protestants in the county.

When I was in college I saw in *Newsweek* a map charting religious distribution across the United States. Red was Protestant and blue was Catholic, and I was not surprised to see that northwestern North Carolina was the most solidly red area in the entire country. Until I was sixteen years old, there was not a single Catholic family in my whole county—and as for Jews, they were as alien as Buddhists. Nor was there much comprehension of these alien persuasions. In 1960, during the Kennedy-Nixon campaign, my mother ran into a respectable Baptist woman in the grocery store. In a lot of ways she liked Kennedy, she said. "But I couldn't vote for him since he's not a Christian."

It's unlikely she would have voted for him anyway. The county was overwhelmingly Republican, nearly 70 percent, which wasn't unusual for southern hill and mountain counties—but sometimes made things rough for my father who was not only school superintendent but also chairman of the county Democratic party. Other than in his brand of politics, however, my father fit in well. He had grown up on a tobacco and dairy farm in the northern part of the county, one of eight brothers and three sisters, and four of his brothers still grew tobacco. Tobacco culture, in fact, dictated the rhythm of county life, from disking and harrowing the soil in late winter and planting in the spring to hoeing and weeding, topping and suckering, priming (i.e., picking) and curing in the summer, to selling in the Winston tobacco market in September and October.

Tobacco barns—small wooden outbuildings that passing-through Yankees often took for living quarters—dotted the landscape. The school calendar was also arranged with tobacco in mind, and August football practice was scheduled for late afternoon after the players—those who lived in the country—got out of the fields. People not only grew tobacco but also many of them worked in Winston-Salem at R. J. Reynolds Tobacco Company

("Reynoldses"), makers of Camels and Winstons and Salems. Every fall the county had a tobacco festival, a tobacco queen. In fact, the only industry Yadkin County had in my childhood was a small tobacco-basket manufacturing plant—billed as the world's largest, though some said it was the only one—in the south end of the county. There was even, as part of the county and regional zeitgeist, what one might call the morality of tobacco: alcohol was bad (at least officially, despite all the moonshiners in the hills), but tobacco was OK for you. I remember, at age nine or ten, a Sunday school class devoted to the proposition that it would be "immoral" to have a job in a brewery. But no one suggested it would be a sin to work at Reynoldses.

If tobacco was the county's economic lifeblood, fast cars were its passion. We were next door to Wilkes after all, right in the heart of early NASCAR country. In most homes Curtis Turner and Lee Petty, Fireball Roberts and Junior Johnson were spoken of as if they were members of the family. Forty or fifty years later, in 2002—less than a year after the Twin Towers attacks as well as the death of NASCAR legend Dale Earnhardt—I recalled just how much that had been, and still was, the case. A folklorist friend of mine, getting responses to September 11 as part of an oral history project in the North Carolina hills, said something to a subject about it having been a bad year. "Yeah," said the subject, "what with Dale and all that shit."

The same thing would have been said in the early 1960s after the death of Fireball Roberts. All of my friends not only had a favorite NASCAR driver but also a favorite *car*—usually the car their favorite driver drove, which was also usually the car their daddy bought—and they defended that car with all the fervor with which I defended Carolina football or basketball. (They could also take the car apart, which is the reason why so many Yadkin County boys went off to North Carolina State and became automotive engineers.) I sometimes went with one of my best friends to dirt-track stock car races, just as he sometimes went with me to Kenan Stadium for Carolina football, and I also went with him up to Mackie's funeral home on occasion to view, in an open casket, the latest would-be Curtis Turner who had wrapped his car around a tree and whose body had been hauled in, dressed up, and put on display. Speed was everything, and I was not fully accepted by some people I knew until, ten days after getting my license at sixteen, I rolled my father's Pontiac on Booger Swamp Road, not exactly racing (it wasn't prearranged) but trying to keep a better driver from passing me. I emerged unscathed, hanging my head in shame at home but hailed as a hero at school.

Not just cars but even highways had a certain mystique. Almost every small town in my county had two major roads meeting in the middle of town, usually at the town's only stoplight, and our two roads were US 421 and 601. Even though 421 was on an east-west tack when it hit Yadkinville, it was in fact a north-south road and went all the way to northern Indiana, running into Lake Michigan just outside Chicago. Just west of town was US 21, which went all the way to Cleveland and Lake Erie. I'd been to Chicago only once and I'd never been to Cleveland, but every time I heard the Indians and White Sox on the radio I imagined 21 and 421 running right up to their ballparks. The rest of the town was equally taken with the romance of the road. Diners and service stations, sometimes even churches, were named for the highways they were on.

Yadkinville: the very name epitomized rural rusticity if not benightedness, an Atlanta friend later told me (he'd known a boy at Davidson College nicknamed "Yadkinville"). Even the mill towns in the area—their textile barons, in a gesture of noblesse oblige, endowing them with YMCAs and swimming pools—tended to look down on it. But, in fact, I liked the place well enough, especially liked my part of town, my street, with huge oaks and maples shading large rambling houses, all built in the late nineteenth and early twentieth century. No antebellum grandeur here, no columns: this was small-town North Carolina, not Mississippi, and it looked more like small-town Ohio or Indiana than the Deep South.

But one thing it did share with the South of legend was a penchant for Gothic. Although my street had only fourteen or fifteen houses on it, in my early years there were in those houses at least three suicides, as well as another violent death or two. When I was about ten, Mr. Branch across the street shot himself one cold morning as I was getting ready for school, and my father was called to their house by his frantic wife. When I was fifteen, Mrs. Gray, three houses up the street, hanged herself in an outbuilding one bright summer day. A year or two later Mr. Johnson, two houses down in the other direction, drove to the town water treatment plant and asphyxiated himself in his car.

This doesn't include the son of the doctor—a doctor himself—two houses up who later, long after I left home, stabbed himself to death, or the next-door neighbor who worked for the town and was killed when a tractor turned over on him. And it doesn't count the next-door neighbor on the other side, the county's Mr. Republican, whose wife came running to our house one Sunday night to summon my father and me, who then went over and found him dead (of natural causes, as it turned out) upright in his chair; or Mr. Wells, just across the street, whose wife also came running for my father when she found her husband in his chair, dead.

And it doesn't take into account all the other trappings of Southern Gothic on the street—William Ball who lived by himself just up the street, who sat in his front porch swing, glared at the children passing by and never seemed to say a word to anyone—our own Boo Radley. Or Donald Wixon, one house down and across the street who was three years older than me and mentally deficient: he was in the habit of knocking on neighbors' doors in the morning and asking if he could come in and make their beds. At the end of the street, also mentally challenged, was a sweet, middle-age man, no taller than five feet, the brother of a leading lawyer in town—and four or five houses up from him a very nice mentally deficient young woman, maybe ten years older than I was, who remained secluded in her house most of the time. Two houses from her was David Brewton, the street's man of letters, who had excelled at Chapel Hill and then at Duke's law school before dropping out, writing a novel, and heading for New York. After several years he had returned to his late mother's rambling Victorian house, lived with his unmarried older sister, grew his hair long, and rode his bicycle twenty-five miles to Winston to play piano at the School of the Arts.

From next door, up the street, came the twangy sounds of country music, then usually called hillbilly music. The sounds came from the Parsons', and it was Mr. Parsons who was later killed by the overturned tractor. He'd married Margaret Phelps, the daughter of old Squire Phelps, one of the richest men in town but a decidedly eccentric one; in Ray Parsons, Margaret had married a man even more eccentric than her father. I lived next door to Ray Parsons for fifteen years, before the tractor turned over on him, and I never heard him say a word, although I did hear, coming across the hedge, grunts and growls directed toward his wife. Mr. Parsons was dark and lean, with long stringy hair, and when he saw me, or any other kid, he just glared. When I later read Mark Twain and encountered Pap Finn, I knew him on the spot—he had lived next door to me all those years.

Not only did his wife love to play country music on the radio, but she played it very loud because she knew my mother didn't like it. Thus I grew up not liking country music either, and I missed out on a lot. I'll bet my father had grown up listening to it, or to what became country music, but my mother set the cultural standards in my house, and that meant classical music or nothing. The Grand Ole Opry, dispensing a rich and lively culture straight from the people, was banned. No bluegrass or honky tonk. I grew up only forty miles from Doc Watson but had never heard of him until a friend, in college in

New England, told me about him when I was twenty-five. Hank Williams was writing and wailing his haunting lyrics, and I think I had barely heard of him, but I didn't know anything about him until I was thirty-five and was filled in by a Jewish friend, originally from Los Angeles.

But, in fact, music — country or classical — meant little to me as I was growing up. Neither was I much of a reader, or at least a reader of what would be called good books, except for a period, in the summer before the fourth grade, when I chain-read a series of orange-bound biographies — *Franklin Roosevelt: Boy of Four Freedoms, Jim Bowie: Boy with a Knife, Jane Addams: Girl of Hull House,* and a couple dozen others which I would take forty or fifty feet up to my perch in a large maple tree in the front yard and read all afternoon. We were the last people on our street to get a television, so I didn't watch much of that, and there was only one movie theater, Crip Shue's, in town. Other than seeing *Song of the South, Samson and Delilah, David and Bathsheba,* and *The African Queen,* I don't remember spending much time there either.

So all there was was sports, and that became virtually my whole life — but such a life, for a ten-year-old, isn't as limiting as it might appear; in fact, it can be downright enlightening. On balance, I'm not sure that reading the sports page from beginning to end, reading in football history books of the exploits of Red Grange, Fielding Yost, Bronko Nagurski, and Amos Alonzo Stagg, collecting baseball cards, and keeping detailed football and basketball scrapbooks — along with my one nonsports obsession, taking the encyclopedia to bed and learning all the state capitals and the nation's top twenty cities in population—was not better training for a future scholar than an early immersion in the Great Books might have been.

I had two sisters, but they were older and saw me as little more than a nuisance, so as far as my interests and activities were concerned I was essentially an only child. When, on summer afternoons, my mother made me go to my room after lunch for an hour or two of reading, I learned all about Brooklyn—which is to say, I turned on the radio and tuned in Nat Albright, who billed himself as "The Voice of the Dodgers." He was no Red Barber or Mel Allen—nor Vin Scully, who was the better-known Voice of the Dodgers—and in fact no one I have met since has ever heard of him. But through Nat Albright I became acquainted with the geography of Brooklyn— with Flatbush, and with Bedford Avenue, which I came to understand was just beyond the right-field fence in Ebbets Field, the territory into which Duke Snider hit towering home runs.

From Nat Albright I also learned the meaning of *voice*, of a personal style. "The bases are FOD, Full of Dodgers," Nat would say, or "FOG, Full of Giants." Snider was "The Duke of Flatbush," and when the count was full Nat would intone, "Count's gone out, gone all the way." Through Nat's commentary I got the flavor of Brooklyn, the meaning of Brooklyn in the nation's imagination. I came to understand that for years people had laughed at it and at the Dodgers—"Dem Bums"—but that others viewed both the borough and its team with great affection. I didn't get to Brooklyn until I was thirty, but when I got there I realized I had been there before. Nat Albright had taken me there.

But why the Dodgers? Why not the Yankees or Red Sox or Giants or Reds? Sports loyalties with kids are strange things. I knew why I was for Carolina, of course, but to this day I can't figure out why a boy in the southern hinterland with no ties whatever to Brooklyn would be for the Dodgers. There were no major-league teams in the South of those days, and a lot of fans in my county were either for the Cardinals—who had a farm team in Winston-Salem—or the Reds, who were geographically closer than any other team (save Washington, which, though first in war and peace, was always last in the American League).

But the Dodgers? I'd like to think it had something to do with breadth of vision and racial tolerance—the Dodgers had signed Jackie Robinson in 1947, and when I became a Dodger fan in the early fifties Brooklyn had a number of other black players, including Roy Campanella, Don Newcombe, and Jim Gilliam—but in fact I'm sure racial tolerance had nothing to do with it at all. The best way I can figure it is that in the early and mid fifties the Yankees and the Dodgers often met in the World Series, and I always saw the Series at the house of a friend who was a big Yankee fan—and friends, at age eight, always being adversaries, I took the other side. And if the Dodgers in the National League, why the Indians in the American? Because, I'm almost certain, of the '54 World Series when the Indians played the Giants, and as a Dodger fan I hated the Giants and thus embraced Vic Wertz, Bob Feller, Bob Lemon, Mike Garcia, Early Wynn, and the rest of the Tribe.

So Nat Albright taught me about Brooklyn, and when I became an Indians fan (although never so much as a Dodger fan) I went to the *Compton's Encyclopedia* and read all about Lake Erie and the Western Reserve and the Cuyahoga River. But even more important than Nat and *Compton's* (other kids had World Book, we had *Compton's*) in my early education were baseball cards. As a formative tool, in fact, it's hard to imagine anything that would have been more valuable for my future line of work. What else—I realized fifteen years later when I was writing my first book—is organizing note cards and envisioning chapters but what I was doing with baseball cards as a boy: categorizing, looking for patterns, seeing what goes with what and what can be changed. And what else is doing an index but a variation of what I had done with baseball cards? I spent hour after hour on rainy summer afternoons, when the Dodgers had an open date and thus weren't on the air, on the floor poring over baseball cards, complete sets of all sixteen major-league teams. Except for Stan Musial of the Cardinals, the Holy Grail of baseball cards: no one could ever get a Stan Musial. Why not, I still don't know.

Those Topps cards (the bubblegum was secondary) gave the team and position of each player, the height and weight, whether he batted and threw left or right, but they also gave the date and place of birth for each player. Based on that information I made trades, and created a team of players born, say, in 1928. Or I made other

trades — Duke Snider for Willie Mays, say, and Carl
Furillo for Hank Aaron, and Karl Spooner for Vinegar
Bend Mizell — and came up with a team of players all
born in Alabama. When I was nine years old my family
had taken a trip across country to Yellowstone and
Glacier Park, and I had some idea what various states
looked like. Through baseball cards and the omnipresent
encyclopedia, I imagined how others would look. What
better education for one who would later try to understand American literature?

Baseball — and football and basketball — taught me geography and history, but they also taught me math, sociology, religion, and much else. Math? I knew without
thinking that 4 for 12 was .333, just as in basketball I
knew in an instant that 17 for 25 from the line was 68 per
cent. More geography? Every Sunday I saw datelines for
football games played in Ann Arbor and Norman and
Ames and Baton Rouge, and to this day (and to what
end?) I know the location and the nickname of every
Division I school in the country. Because three of my favorite Carolina basketball players were from Hoboken,
Bayonne, and Bergenfield, New Jersey, I looked up on
the map those municipalities, learned their populations,
romanticized them (then deromanticized them twenty
years later when I saw the actual places), wondered what
they were like. Through the players' hometowns recorded
on a roster I came to be fascinated with place, and place
as shaper of self, a fascination that still lasts. A few years
ago, as I drove north on the West Virginia Turnpike, I
sought out Cabin Creek to see the beginnings of the legend of Jerry West. Another time, when I was driving up

the west bank of the Mississippi toward St. Louis, I went through Crystal City to see the hometown of Bill Bradley. Through French Lick, Indiana, for Larry Bird. Through Beaver Falls, Pennsylvania, for Joe Namath. Why not, as long as I was in the area?

Sociology and religion? Easy. As a southerner I knew only black and white, but when I saw the basketball rosters in the Atlantic Coast Conference — Maglio, Molodet, Stephanovich, Kalbfus, Bukowsky, Lakata, Seitz — I realized there were different kinds of white. I didn't know a Pole from a German from an Italian, but I had my father explain why these names weren't Johnson and Davis and Williams. As for religion, my favorite Carolina team ever started four Irish Catholics and a Jew — Brennan, Quigg, Kearns, Cunningham, and Rosenbluth — all from New York City or its outskirts. My entire county, as I think I've said, had not a single one of either. I think I had been introduced to religious tolerance before that, but if not it came at that moment, in 1957. Before Kennedy, for me, there were Brennan and Kearns and Quigg.

And most of all, race. If I didn't become a Dodger fan because they had Robinson and Campy and Newcombe and Gilliam, I certainly came to admire them *because* they were Dodgers — and Robinson because he was the classiest and the guttiest of them all. This was the early 1950s South, remember, even before 1954 and *Brown v. Board of Education,* and a southern child didn't *ever* see black and white people of any sort compete — or interact in any fashion — on the same stage. My Tar Heels didn't have any black players; neither did any other southern teams. So when I read that Pee Wee Reese (a white Kentuckian) had befriended Robinson, and when I saw the other black Dodgers—and Willie Mays of the Giants and Ernie Banks of the Cubs—joking around with white players before or after the game, that told me integration (though I wouldn't necessarily have called it that) could work. When I saw the San Francisco Dons, with Bill Russell and K. C. Jones, win two NCAA basketball titles in the mid-fifties—when I saw Oscar Robertson at Cincinnati and Wilt Chamberlain at Kansas win with grace and style—that told me something too. Sure, this was just athletics, and what I didn't see was that Russell and Jones and Robertson and Wilt were still turned away from restaurants and hotels, sometimes in the North as well as the South. But I learned that at least in some parts of the country, and at least in one arena, the arena I valued most, they competed as equals.

So sports were partly about education, I can now see, but I certainly didn't think they were about education then. To me they were just about fun and excitement, about action, about competing, staying in motion—at least on a summer's day—from morning until you were called in for supper at night. That's what I lived for, from about age eight on, and what I realized even then—but realize even more now—is that I was very lucky to be able to play at all. For when I was five years old I had had polio, a case that put me in the hospital for two weeks. About half of the people who entered the hospital with polio in the late 1940s and early 1950s walked out on their own. About half did not.

I've now gone more than fifty years hardly thinking

about polio, yet it could easily have changed my life altogether, not to mention ended it. The nation has experienced a similar amnesia. After Jonas Salk and Albert Sabin and the vaccines of the 1950s, polio was pronounced "cured"—rather, prevented—in this country, and it is now as forgotten (except by those who still make their way with braces and crutches, and by aging sufferers of post-polio syndrome) as the great influenza epidemic of 1918 was by, say, 1950. But at its peak, largely the mid-1940s to the early 1950s, polio was the Great National Scourge—along with Communism, of course. And like McCarthyism, with which it shared an era, it created panic, a sort of national hysteria, the fear of an enemy out there that could not be identified, let alone conquered. As one historian of polio has written, it "was terror. Overwhelming, gut-wrenching terror . . . The Dread Disease. . . . The AIDS of the middle of the twentieth century." Every summer in the late 1940s and early 1950s parents knew what was coming. Public officials closed swimming pools, playgrounds, movie theaters, summer camps—and still polio came, always hitting its peak in late summer and then declining when the first frost hit. During the epidemic, houses (including mine) were quarantined, neighbors hesitated to talk with neighbors, children were sent out of town to the country—all of which rarely did any good.

   Given that I was hit in the summer of 1948, during the worst polio epidemic in North Carolina history, you'd think my hometown doctor would have suspected something when my parents called him to our house to examine me. They had known something was wrong when I was unable to bow my head during grace before supper. The doctor came, took note of my high fever, headache, stiff neck, aching back and legs—and diagnosed flu. My parents, suspecting something more sinister, took me down to Baptist Hospital in Winston-Salem where a spinal tap confirmed the diagnosis of polio. I can't remember a great deal about the next two weeks, but I do remember being put in a ward with a dozen or so other children. I remember going to a treatment room two or three times a day, being wrapped in hot, wet pads resembling blankets, and then having my legs and back massaged. I remember—as a diversionary tactic—they give me all the chocolate milk I wanted.

All the descriptions of polio wards I have read paint a pretty terrifying picture: children screaming in pain, parents weeping, the constant sound of iron lungs whooshing and pumping ("the background music for the polio experience," one historian has written) and the wet packs "as hot as you could stand." But I remember little of that—not even extreme discomfort from the hot packs in a hospital without air-conditioning in the middle of a southern summer. I don't recall any great pain, although I must have had it—and I was too young to have any awareness of possible debilitating consequences. I recall my parents coming to visit every day (although I've read that parents were often banned from the wards), late in the afternoon, and all I remember is that they were as calm and reassuring as they always were—although certainly *they* were aware of negative consequences.

For, in truth, there was little the doctors could do, except, in certain cases, keep people alive to face permanent paralysis, and, in less severe cases, make people comfortable. None of the therapy really helped: it might loosen muscles that were going to make it through anyway, but nothing could prevent—or reverse—the paralysis. It was determinism at its worst: either you were going to be paralyzed or you weren't. Some kids died shortly after reaching the hospital. Some—with bulbar polio, the kind that affected respiration—were placed in the dreaded iron lung. Others had legs and other limbs paralyzed. And others, including me, endured the hot packs and the massages for a few weeks and then walked out of the hospital.

When I got home, I remember, I had to rest a lot, and I recall not being able to sleep some nights, because of restlessness. The rest of that summer, I remember, I kept hearing in the very early morning, at first light, the melancholy coos of a mourning dove in the woods behind the house—an eerie sound that frightened me greatly and about the only thing in my mind, other than chocolate milk, that I still connect to polio. But within several months of getting out of the hospital I was fully back on my feet, back to running, back to swimming and riding my bicycle, climbing Grandfather Mountain with my parents and sisters, and after a year or two it seemed as if polio had never happened. Except that—in the four or five summers still left of the polio panic, before Salk and then Sabin put an end to it, those four or five summers when parents and children still waited in fear—I felt pretty special, *untouchable:* I had had it and couldn't get it again. (Or so we were told at the time.) Every time I saw Harold Long, a boy four years older than I was, shuffling along with his braces and crutches, I remembered: he had been in the hospital the same summer I was.

That's why I was lucky to be playing sports at all. I'm not sure polio had anything to do with why I took to football and basketball and baseball with such passion, but once I recovered that's all I was interested in. And not only those mainstream sports. For a year or so, when I was ten, I was totally absorbed in Roger Bannister and his breaking of the four-minute mile—realizing, even then I think, that this was and might continue to be the most important moment in sports in the twentieth century. (When I discovered forty years later that one of my academic colleagues, as an Oxford undergraduate, had actually been at the meet, had been one of the five hundred people to see Bannister break the impossible barrier that gray spring afternoon, I viewed him with awe, as if he had been present at the creation.) But for some reason when, later that spring in Vancouver, Bannister, the medical student, one of the last pure amateurs, met the Australian John Landy (who had also broken four minutes just after Bannister) in the Mile of the Century, I was for Landy, not Bannister. The Aussie became my hero, and I took to the country roads around my town, running, imagining I was John Landy.

But mainly it was basketball—not just coinciding with but directly related to the demise of Carolina football and the coming to Chapel Hill of Frank McGuire, the sweet-talking basketball coach from Brooklyn. Up until that point basketball in North Carolina had been dominated by N.C. State, whose own coach, Everett Case, had come down from Indiana in the mid-1940s, brought with him Hoosier recruits, built the largest basketball arena in the South (called—what else?—The House that Case Built), and was winning everything in sight. Carolina was not bad, but Skippy Winstead, Paul Likins, Bud Maddie—*those* names would never shake down the thunder from on high or rest in the rafters of the Dean Dome. But when McGuire, fresh from winning the Eastern Regionals at St. John's, came to Chapel Hill—bringing *his* players, largely Irish Catholics, from New York—the battle was joined. The Atlantic Coast Conference was born, and what was to be acclaimed the fiercest hoops competition in the country—Carolina, State, Duke, and Wake Forest, at that time all within thirty miles of each other—was under way.

The appeal to a ten-year-old kid in western North Carolina, in a town that seemed to offer nothing to do, was immeasurable. Basketball was it. My father—as I've said, not particularly crazy about sports himself, but seeing that I was—took half of the backyard and made me a fifty-foot court, with baskets at each end, and that's where I spent all my afternoons after school, as well as most Saturdays and holidays, from November till March. At first the court was all grass, but after one season most of it, particularly the areas around each goal, had become hard dirt, perfect for dribbling. There was only one thing wrong with the court—a pile of scrap boards, nails sticking out of some of them, just beyond the east goal. Why my father, who had gone to a lot of trouble to put up the goals, did not move the scrap pile I don't know. Why *I* didn't, I don't know—other than my lifelong inability to realize that one's physical environment can be altered. In any case, in battles for rebounds under the basket—or at the end of a fast break, punctuated by a hard foul—you could easily fall into the lumber pile. At least twice I stumbled or was pushed into the pile and stepped on a nail, another time snagged my finger on one, and each time ended up in the emergency room.

Hard fouls were part of the game. Junior Noble and Jackie Goss were older and tougher than I was, and Johnny Crater was much bigger and stronger. His father had been a high school star twenty years earlier, and he knew how to use elbows even at age ten. Jackie, a sweet kid with a lot of tough friends, often brought them along and a lot of us ended up in the lumber pile. Grady Dalton's father had spent some time in the pen. So had Jerry Snipes's father, after he had shot Jerry's mother. Billy Atkins had just moved to town from Florida and before that had lived in California; a good-looking kid with that glamorous background, he stole my girlfriend for a time—until her parents discovered the California and Florida sojourns had been for migratory farm work. All of these kids played tough, and that's what I needed. I was a shooter but, at first, little else. At age eleven I had been sent to YMCA camp in the mountains and, since all the other campers were from other and larger towns, I'd suffered a bad case of homesickness—only to be cured when I won the all-camp free throw championship, hitting 21 of 25 and knocking off a fourteen-year-old boy in the finals.

Although for a time my backyard court was a kind of gathering place, basketball at first was not primarily a social activity for me. It was mostly a solitary one, which was the way I wanted it. Most afternoons after school and most Saturdays I had the court to myself. I practiced shots from all angles, did dribbling drills up and down the court, but what I did mainly was play the upcoming Carolina games. That is, I would play the *whole* game. I knew who Carolina was to play next, and I did my research in the sports pages of the *Winston-Salem Journal*, learning the names and positions of all the other team's starters. If the opponent was State or Duke or Wake, I already knew them.

I had already learned the style and cadences of the radio voice of the Tar Heels — actually he was principally the voice of the N. C. State Wolfpack, but I liked his style so I claimed him for the Tar Heels — and I often went around declaiming his opening words, which I remember to this day: "Good evening, ladies and gentlemen, this is Ray Reeve, speaking to you once again from the basketball capital of the South, the William Neal Reynolds Coliseum, on the campus of North Carolina State College, here in Raleigh, North Carolina [PAUSE] . . . where TONIGHT the Wolfpack, coached by the Ol' Gray Fox, Everett Case, is proud to play host to the Tar Heels of the University of North Carolina, coached by Frank Mc-Guire."

Then I would announce the starting lineups — shifting, as Ray Reeve always did, to the public-address announcer, C. A. Dillon, Jr., who would introduce the starters in his dulcet tones: "For the Tar Heels, at left forward, at six feet five inches, from the Bronx, Number 10, Lennie Rosenbluth . . ." and so on. I had mastered, as had many other schoolboys, a guttural sound that resembled the roar of the crowd, and for Rosenbluth it lasted a long time.

The game itself I would both play and announce, taking every shot, getting every rebound, positioning myself on the court as I passed the ball around—to myself. "To Vayda in the right-hand corner, to Radovich at the top of the key, who feeds Rosenbluth flashing into the lane. . . . It's GOOOOD." More roar. And so it went, forty minutes, with a break for halftime (scoring totals and halftime commentary thrown in). Of course, the game always came out the right way: the Heels always won. When they were playing Clemson or Virginia it wasn't even close. If State or Wake (Duke didn't seem much of a threat in those days), it was always close at the end. Usually Carolina trailed by one with five seconds left and Rosenbluth—I—took the last shot, usually a jumper from the left corner. If it went in, great—we won. If it didn't, Rosenbluth was fouled on the play and went to the line for two. If he—I—hit both, we still won. If he missed, Ron Shavlik of the Wolfpack had stepped in the lane too early and Rosenbluth got another. If he missed again (unlikely), Joe Quigg—I—tapped it in. We couldn't lose.

I don't know what the neighbors thought of all this. A weird kid, obviously. Why isn't he raking leaves? Hauling wood? Out under a car somewhere? And who is this Rosenbluth? This Radovich? This Shavlik? Doesn't sound like any names around here. I don't even know what my parents thought. But, again, I wouldn't take anything for it. I was involved in history, *creating my own narrative*—what better activity for one who would someday try to be a writer?

I don't know how good I was in those early days—
there was no organized basketball in my town before the
seventh grade, and by then I was already starting to lose
the growth contest. I'd towered over Jimmy Dobbins in
the fourth and fifth grades; now he was 5'8". Michael
Adams was 5'10". Johnny Crater was almost six feet.
And I was 5'4". Someone should write a treatise—someone may already have—on how height in those uncertain
years affects basketball psyches. I'd been a relatively big
boy, and now I was a shrimp. Sure I could shoot and
could handle the ball, but I couldn't rebound. I had my
mother take me to an orthopedist—who came up with a
diagnosis that had nothing to do with my problem ("tight
heel bands," he said, whatever that meant) but his remedy, arch supports, added a half inch to my height.

I sought hope wherever I could find it. I remember the
Wake Forest coach, Bones McKinney, stopping by one
Sunday afternoon to talk with my father about some
school matter. They were sitting on the front porch when
I came up, and my father happened to mention to Bones
that I was worried I'd never grow. "Let me see your feet,"
Bones commanded. I held one up for him to inspect.
"You'll grow to at least 6'2"," he said. "And when you do,
you'll be better because you'll have developed little man
skills"—by which he meant shooting, ball-handling, gen-
eral court sense. He was right, at least about the growing.
But it was to take a long time.

What I *could* do, I realized, was jump—which didn't
help me much at 5'4" but, I figured, would help me a lot if
I ever started to grow. I had some inkling of this new-
found talent back in Yadkinville, but it was tested—certi-

fied—only when I went to Durham to spend a few days with some friends, three brothers, all near my age. Their father taught at Duke, and they lived near the campus, so we had access on those summer afternoons to Duke Indoor Stadium (later renamed, and glorified in college basketball circles as the most famous basketball court in the land, the notorious Cameron Fieldhouse), and I was happy to discover I was somewhat on the level of my friend Win, who had made a name for himself in Durham junior basketball circles. Five or six years later Win would head off to boarding school at Andover, where he would achieve prominence as a three-sport star and would room with a perennial bench-warmer, George W. Bush, whose skills were more tailored for cheerleading than for hoop. In the Andover basketball team photo, circa 1964, Win, as captain, sits in the middle with the ball in his hand; Bush, the athlete wannabe, stands, banished to the far corner of the back row.

But that lay ahead. In 1956 Win had only the Carr Junior High team in his sights, and I went with him one day to a basketball clinic at Durham High School, conducted by one of the state's best coaches, Simon Terrell. One of Terrell's drills was a jumping competition, measuring what now would be called vertical leap—a test, unrelated to height, which measures how far you can get off the floor, not how high you can touch. Until that moment I had done nothing remarkable to distinguish myself in the eyes of Simon Terrell or the big-city Durham boys. I had been decidedly mediocre. But in jumping I beat them all—older guys, taller guys, better guys. I was the champion vertical leaper.

Why? they asked. The theory finally agreed upon was that it probably had something to do with my rural origins. Until then I had thought of myself as almost *urban* — which is to say, in the particular dialectic of Yadkin County, I was definitely a town boy, as opposed to a country boy who lived on a farm and rode the bus to school. But, in Durham, I was decidedly rural — and I could jump. The reason, the cognoscenti of Carr Junior High concluded, was that, being rural, I probably worked in the fields all day, and the field work — all the bending and stretching and lifting — had doubtless developed my legs. Thirty years later Jimmy the Greek would be fired from CBS for saying approximately the same thing about black athletes, or at least their ancestors. I hadn't worked a day in my life in the fields, but I wasn't complaining. Labeling — abstracting — is what happens when you leave Yadkinville and encounter Durham and the larger world, and there it was: I was a country boy and I was a vertical leaper.

3

Democrats and Methodists

When I was a boy, the world seemed to me a kind of morality play. There was good and bad, or at least less good. Operating as a kind of Trinity were the Democratic Party, the Methodist Church, and—at least as I saw it—the Carolina Tar Heels. Each of my parents exercised dominion over one point of the Trinity, and I the third. Which is to say: My religion was basketball, my father's was politics, and my mother's was, well, religion—though hardly the southern-fried brand of Billy Graham.

My father's leanings were known to almost everyone in the county. His dual position as superintendent of schools and chairman of the county Democratic Party is a combination that would undoubtedly be impossible today, and one that constituted a kind of juggling act even in his own time. His school position, in a strongly Republican county, was made possible only by the fact that the school board was appointed, not elected, and that the appointments were made by the largely Democratic General Assembly in Raleigh—which meant that the county school board was, at least for the first twenty years of his tenure, all Democratic. The county board in turn appointed and retained the superintendent. My father's reasoning was that an appointed, as opposed to an elected, school board meant that politics were kept out of the schools. Well . . . to me that had a certain logic.

Because of his Democratic activism and his thirty-three years as school superintendent, my father achieved a certain prominence, even minor legendary status, in the county. The *Yadkin Ripple*, a strongly Republican newspaper, found him a favorite target, and people in many quarters, although always calling him "Mr. Hobson" to his face, simply referred to him as "Fred C." He was tall—6'3"—and when the county had a heavy snowfall, some people (my friends later told me) described the depth as "ass deep to Fred Hobson." I'd always heard "ass deep to Boone Harding," a prominent, and equally tall, Republican lawyer in the county, but it makes sense I wouldn't have heard the other until later.

Fred C., though as Tar Heel as you could get, had actually been born in California, in April 1906 just north of San Francisco, and thus was eight days old when the earthquake hit. According to my grandmother, his cradle rocked from one side of the upstairs nursery to the other but didn't turn over. My grandparents had gone west just after their marriage in 1905 for adventure and fortune; whether it was the earthquake or something else that chased them out, they came back to North Carolina shortly after my father's birth, and my grandfather took over some family land and set to farming.

In 1925 they sent their oldest son off to Chapel Hill, a hundred miles downstate, just at the time Carolina—

which had recently been the first state university in the late Confederacy to name a Yankee president—was becoming the leading, and by far the most liberal, university in the South. The university, which numbered among its recent graduates Thomas Wolfe and Sam Ervin, was amassing an impressive faculty for a heretofore provincial and isolated southern school. Particularly important for my father was his history professor, Frank Porter Graham, a native North Carolinian who was committed to racial justice and the gospel of public service. Fred C. got into Democratic politics early, making his way over to Raleigh to attend an Al Smith rally in the fall of 1928. Moved by Smith's stump speech, he then cast his first vote later that fall for Smith, the wet Catholic from New York.

Though he never lived on a farm again, my father remained a farm boy at heart. He was big and strong—huge hands and size 14 shoes—and he liked to work outside more than anything else; he said it's what he did instead of golf. Or what he did instead of any other sport: although he put up my goals in the backyard, I never saw him shoot a basket in his life, nor throw a football or a baseball. What he did do, year after year, was plant the biggest vegetable garden in town, more than a hundred feet long and sixty or seventy feet across, and when he came home from work on summer days he would go straight to the garden, still in his suit, to check on the progress of corn and tomatoes and beans and cantaloupes. On summer Saturday afternoons when political cronies would come by, they would know to find him in the garden. I remember seeing them there, standing in the sun, pondering gravely who they'd put up for county commissioner or tax collector while Fred C. leaned on his hoe. It was not quite the same as Senator LeRoy Percy of Mississippi receiving political allies on the veranda with mint juleps, Delta style—as reported by Will Percy in *Lanterns on the Levee*—but something more appropriate for the Carolina hill country.

My father was a farm boy too in his understanding of the processes, and disregard of the dangers, of the natural world. I remember being impressed as a young boy—a town boy would be—when seeing him take an axe and behead a chicken for dinner. Later I was astounded at the way he would climb a ladder to the eaves of the house and, with a gloved hand, pull down a wasp nest and throw it out into the yard below, wasps trailing behind the nest but not a one lighting on him. He had that same disregard of danger—or maybe that sense of *expendability* in regard to children that comes from being one of eleven—when it came to me too. He let me climb the highest trees around and, at other times, had me dangling from the roof cleaning gutters when I was pretty certain I would fall—things few parents would ever risk today. As a country boy, he believed in corporal punishment, not only in his schools but also in his home: the childhood moment I feared most was seeing him going out to a backyard tree or bush, picking off a switch, and heading back to the house with me as his target. He was always conscious of his rough-hewn origins and altogether comfortable with them. When one of my sisters went through a phase of labeling certain things "country," he looked more puzzled and hurt than angry. "What's *wrong* with country?" he'd say.

He may have remained a farm boy, but he also had a certain sense of decorum and propriety that came from his years at Chapel Hill or perhaps from trying to impress my mother in their early courting days. There was something of the rural English gentleman in him, the educated man who felt most comfortable on the land. He believed in dressing well, which he interpreted as meaning that every man should have at least three or four Harris Tweed sports coats in his closet, as well as a good Harris Tweed overcoat that would last a lifetime. He wouldn't touch a cigarette, but he smoked a pipe as he sat in his study, the aroma of Sir Walter Raleigh tobacco filling the house. His speech was spotted with rather antiquated English pronunciations—"a-tall" (for "at all"), "goo-deal" (for "good deal"), "li'-bry," and so forth—which were not affectations but rather country English speech brought to these shores a couple of centuries earlier.

He was also the most precise grammarian I have ever known, and the one most likely to jump on someone, at least in his own family, who wasn't. "*What?*" he would explode when he heard, even in the next room, a dangling participle or the nominative case being used in the objective. He kept a dictionary both in the den and the kitchen, and he challenged anyone who used a word incorrectly. The same philosophy of getting it right also applied to firm handshakes and shining shoes. His standard of conduct was hard to meet. "What has he contributed?" he would ask about any young man my sisters, in college and later, brought home for inspection—by which he meant, what has he contributed to his *community*, to society, in the way of public service. Not how much money he made, or stood to make. Not what his father did. Not where he went to school. But what had he contributed—what *good* was he? And he was equally ready to challenge me on any excuse I might make. "I didn't mean to," I would say. "You didn't mean *not* to," he would counter. "Jimmy Dobbins got to do it," I would say. "You're not Jimmy Dobbins," he would answer.

All this might suggest that my father was overly demanding, and in many ways he was. But he was also one of the happiest, as well as one of the most confident and unself-conscious, people I have ever met. He would rise early each morning and prowl through the house, awakening us all by quoting the Chaucer he had memorized in his sophomore year at Chapel Hill—"Whan that Aprill with his shoures soote/The droghte of March hath perced to the roote/And bathed every veyne in swich licour/Of which vertu engendred is the flour"—always arriving at my room just as he got to "the tendre croppes and the *yonge sonne.*"

My father was also one of the happiest workers I ever saw—which is to say, one of the few people I've known who made absolutely no distinction between work and fun. Work *was* fun, he said, and I think he meant it, both his duties in the superintendent's office and—all day long, on summer Saturdays, in the sun—in the garden. Early summer mornings, before heading to the office, you could see him going from house to house on our street, putting on everyone's front porches what he had just picked or dug. I asked him why he didn't sell what we didn't need, and he said it would take the fun away.

He was to have fun with the garden until his mideighties, still tilling, planting, hoeing, watering, and picking until my mother died and he decided he couldn't stay alone in the house they had shared for fifty-five years. He himself would die within a year. When, a couple of years later, I went back to Yadkinville and drove by the old place, I found where once had been a hundred feet of garden nothing but featureless green lawn—not a sign that for more than a half century that ground had yielded tomatoes and corn and squash and beans for an entire street.

Despite his generosity, my father was, finally, a man of his generation—and in this, I think, not just a rural man of his generation—in his inability to express his feelings, particularly to his son. Friends whose parents were younger than mine (he was in his late thirties when I was born) have sometimes been astounded when I tell them that my father never hugged me, never said he loved me—although he showed me he did in any number of ways. I happened to realize in his last few months of life that I'd probably never told him either, so I tried it, with near comic results. "I love you," I said, as he sat there, dressed in his favorite flannel shirt, in a wheelchair. "Thank you," he replied, politely, formally. I tried again a couple of days later. "I love you, Dad." "Thank you," he said again. Nothing, not even the shadow of death, was going to make him *tell* his son he loved him. "Thank you" was as much as I ever got, and it was only one of several expressions from his last years that came to define him more clearly in my mind—a man somewhat formal, eminently practical. When he had turned eighty—in good health, with nine more years to live—he started telling his children at Christmas, "Don't give me any clothes. I've got enough for the duration." Every Christmas for eight years he repeated: "I've got enough for the duration." And he did.

But as I was about to say about my father's political leanings, before the talk about his background and convictions broke in . . . Or maybe they did not break in at all since those qualities I was talking about—his idealism mixed with a certain practicality, his commitment to public service, his egalitarianism (though mixed with a bit of old-style paternalism), not to mention an inheritance from parents who were themselves strong Wilsonian Democrats—made him in the 1930s a classic FDR liberal, at least its southern variety. (As for his work ethic—he would have said—Democrats can have that too.) In any case, when he came back to Yadkin County in 1939, school superintendency or not, he plunged into politics.

Fred C. became—already was—a Yellow Dog Democrat of the purest breed: in his sixty-eight years as a registered voter he would never once vote for a Republican, and he never let his children forget that our mother had once, in a local election when she was in her twenties, cast one vote for the GOP. He thought politically at every level. As a kid, I knew the political affiliation of almost everyone in town—simply because, if I should ask about anyone (no matter what the subject), my father would be likely to begin, "Well, he's a good Democrat," or "He's a

Republican." Except there were two sorts of Republicans: "He's a Republican you can work with" or "He's a no-good Republican"—which I took to mean, one you couldn't work with.

Of course, in Yadkin County it was hopeless—the Democrats hadn't won a single county office in the twentieth century—but that didn't keep him from trying and hoping. Every election day he sent out a cadre of drivers, including me once I hit sixteen, to pick up registered Democrats in remote parts of the county and bring them in. He hovered on the perimeter of the polling place, greeting and passing out campaign literature to voters as they piled out of the car. After the polls closed he walked home for supper, then always back to the courthouse to look on as the votes were counted. About midnight he trudged home, and we heard him come in the house. The results were always the same. Except, finally, once. In 1958 the voters, angry that the Republican county commissioners had torn down the antebellum courthouse and replaced it with an unsightly new one, voted out the Republicans and voted in a whole slate of Democrats, county commissioners, sheriff, and all. It was the first— and was to be the only—Democratic victory of the twentieth century in Yadkin County. But I can't recall that Dad's response was terribly different that night. I think he was so resigned to defeat, at least on the local level, that he didn't know how to react any other way.

So devoted was my father to the Democratic Party that he even planned family vacations around politics. When we went on a long western trip in 1952, he made sure we would pass through Springfield, Illinois, just at the time Adlai Stevenson came back from winning the nomination at the Democratic convention. We were right there for the downtown rally. The year before, we had taken our family vacation to Washington to see not only historical sites but also the Senate and House in session. Our congressman, C. B. Deane—four years later voted out of office for refusing to sign the pro-segregationist Southern Manifesto—always stayed with us when he was visiting Yadkin County, unsuccessfully trolling for votes in those inhospitable waters, and, in Washington, he took us down to the floor of the House and introduced me to Sam Rayburn, the Speaker.

All during that trip to Washington, I recall, my sisters and I—and, I suppose, my father—had been after my mother to call her old college boyfriend, Charlie Murphy, who was now President Truman's chief speechwriter. They had been close—he had been my Uncle Bob's roommate at Duke, and she had been pinned to Murphy for a time—but she hadn't seen him in twenty years and didn't want to call. Finally, as we were leaving town, she gave in—and Murphy said to come on over to the White House. We arrived, got admitted, and he showed us all around, ending up in the Oval Office. Truman wasn't in, but Charlie Murphy said I could sit in the president's chair, and I did. I remembered being a little frightened. This was only a few months after two Puerto Rican nationalists had attempted to assassinate Truman, and at age eight I figured someone would be after him again and might get me by mistake. I remember only that—and the fact that Charlie Murphy, though he let me sit in the president's chair, didn't ask my sisters to.

The year before I sat in Truman's chair, I had had my view of the world as morality play reinforced by an election that would go down as North Carolina's fiercest and dirtiest of the twentieth century—and the election that would cause my father more pain than any other. His old history professor, Frank Graham, who had gone on to become president of the University of North Carolina and was the closest thing to a racial integrationist that southern politics could find in 1950, faced off in the Democratic primary (*that*, of course, was the real election in those days) for a U.S. Senate seat against a staunch segregationist named Willis Smith, whose chief strategist was twenty-eight-year-old Jesse Helms, then news director for WRAL radio in Raleigh. After Graham handily won the first primary, but Smith got enough votes to call for a runoff, the stage was set for a race-baiting assault against Graham, the worst in Tar Heel history. In a bitter campaign that featured, among other things, a doctored photograph of Graham's wife dancing with a black soldier, Smith won and went off to the U.S. Senate. Graham bowed out, not altogether broken but finished as a force in North Carolina politics—a small, sweet man with unyielding convictions and integrity, becoming in time a kind of martyr, a sort of Tar Heel Gandhi. In that 1950 campaign my father saw that the issue of race, never before a decisive factor in North Carolina politics (*all* whites had been segregationists), was here to stay as the dominant issue. What he didn't know was that he would be seeing Graham's nemesis Jesse Helms for another half century.

I barely remember the Graham-Smith fight, just the tone

and mood in our house during that period, but I had become a kind of junior activist in my own right by the time
of the Eisenhower-Stevenson presidential campaigns of
1952 and 1956. I wore Stevenson campaign badges, fought
I Like Ike advocates, and put Stevenson bumper stickers
on Republican cars (the latter without my father's knowledge). But what I remember most was *Brown v. Board of
Education* in May 1954, eleven days after Roger Bannister
broke the four-minute mile. I was out in the woods, looking for arrowheads with my buddy Red Royall, when
Red—heretofore not a student of Supreme Court deci-
sions—suddenly turned on me and charged: "Your daddy's
gonna make us go to school with niggers." I denied it—
said *he* wasn't responsible—but that didn't shake Red.
When we went by his house later that afternoon he introduced me to his mother: "This is Freddy. His daddy owns
the schoolhouse. He's gonna make us go to school with
niggers." The rest of the county apparently thought the
same thing. Later that month a school bond election my
father had been pushing for more than a year—*this* time,
after several earlier rejections, it had looked like the voters might finally give him enough money to improve the
schools—went down to a crushing defeat.

That was the pattern for the 1950s. Ike always won—
after the landslide of 1952, the avalanche in 1956—and
race was to be the issue in the South for the next three
decades, if not longer. I was to find redemption only in
1960—with Kennedy and, in North Carolina, the victory
of Terry Sanford, still seen as the most liberal Tar Heel
governor ever. My father may have believed in the separation of church and state, but not schools and state: I re-

member when Sanford campaigned in Yadkin County, Dad had him there in his superintendent's office, greeting all comers. But after 1960, and especially 1964, it was clear that the entire order was changing. With Democratic defections over race (even Jesse Helms had been a Democrat at first), the GOP was on the rise, both in North Carolina and across the South. To my father, politically speaking, Dixie was beginning to look like Yadkin County writ large: Republicans everywhere. He didn't like it but he could take it if he had to. He'd been there all his life.

On the surface, you might not have thought my father and mother would be altogether compatible. Unlike my father, the farm boy with no particular sense of the importance of his family roots, my mother frequently summoned up long-gone Tuttles and Gregorys as if they were still part of the human landscape. All sides of her family had been in the South since 1800, but she was still aware of old New England roots on one side—in fact, was proud of nothing more than the fact she had come from the early Tuttles of Massachusetts and Connecticut, that her direct ancestor William Tuttle had been a founder of New Haven, that Yale University (as she had discovered in the Yale archives) had been built in part on William Tuttle's land, and that Jonathan Edwards's grandmother, Elizabeth Tuttle, had also been her several-times-great grandmother too. My father made fun of all this—he had that country boy's debunking confidence—and he preferred to look ahead, not to the past. He came from a family in which most of the boys, if they went to college at all, went to N.C. State to pursue practical disciplines such as engineering and animal husbandry—unlike the Tuttles who had attended college since the mid–nineteenth century, had gone to Duke and Vanderbilt, and had studied such arcane things as literature and theology. Mother's first cousin wound up as head of the World Methodist Council; Dad's brother ended up the world's foremost authority on Jersey cows.

It's a pattern I've observed in a great number of southern families, particularly those that produce academics and writers—that is, this matter of women being from a higher social station than their husbands. It must all even out in the end, but it's astounding the number of subjects I've come across whose parents fit this pattern, though I don't think I've ever seen anyone really investigate the matter. Once, in doing research for a book that treated some dozen and a half southern writers, I discovered that at least 80 percent of their parents followed the pattern—and my dozen or so subjects for a second book repeated it. In my own family, I've noticed the same thing, both sides, for three generations back.

Just why, I'm not sure. In most cases—and certainly in the case of my own family—it had nothing to do with money. Neither side had much. Could it have been rather that, especially in the southern mythos, women were associated with refinement, high culture, and social respectability, and an ambitious, hard-working young man would want those qualities in a wife more than he would want money?—which, after all, being hard-working and ambitious, he would soon accumulate anyway. Men, on the other hand, did not have to be refined and cultivated to be good catches for proper southern women; they could have rough edges, just so they were solid, were headed for success, and were guaranteed to make good providers.

In any event, in the case of my parents, it worked out beautifully. It was as if each felt superior to the other in some realm—my father in the public sphere, as a player in county and regional affairs; my mother in the private sphere, as moral arbiter, having a sense of inner worth that did not have to be reinforced by the outside world. On almost all things they agreed, although often—originally—for different reasons. If anything, my mother's politics were more liberal than my father's, but then she wouldn't have referred to her set of social beliefs as "politics" at all. His pantheon would have included Andrew Jackson, Woodrow Wilson, Franklin Roosevelt, and Harry Truman; hers Gandhi, Eleanor Roosevelt, Albert Schweitzer—and Jesus Christ. They differed only in that my father's idealism was always tempered by pragmatism, and hers, generally speaking, was not. She, for example, would have integrated the Yadkin County schools (or would have tried) on the spot, in 1954, if she had been superintendent, while my father—aware of the explosiveness of the situation even in a county with a population that was less than 10 percent African American—paid a little more attention to the adjective in "with all deliberate speed."

The interesting thing about my parents—particularly to me, since I would later spend a good part of my career writing about the South—is that, in my mind, they were never very identifiably southern at all, at least not in the way the myth would have it. Although their families on all sides had been in the South for at least a century and a half, had all fought for the Confederacy and had (in the case of the Tuttles and Gregorys, though not the Hobsons) been slaveholders—and though my parents spoke with southern accents, loved southern cooking and southern storytelling, and admired Robert E. Lee as a "gentleman"—they were not those southerners of legend, freewheeling, hard-drinking, given (as Mississippian William Alexander Percy would put it) to the good life. My father did not hunt or fish (no moral objections—he just didn't have time), didn't even own a gun, didn't drink bourbon, and neither parent subscribed to fundamentalist religion or conservative politics.

I think the reason is that, at some deep level, they never fully took to the South: that their particular heritages—my father's Quaker one, my mother's Puritan— stuck with them, even after more than a century, and that a certain Quaker-Puritan propensity for high thinking and plain living remained. I have often thought it somewhat strange that I myself, who would later spend much time pondering the ways of the South, would come of age so thoroughly disapproving both of the southern anthem "Dixie" and the Confederate flag, and I'm sure my parents (as well as the fact that both "Dixie" and the battle flag were used as symbols of segregation when I was a kid) are largely the reason why. I'm not sure they actually *said* anything, but I must have sensed their disapproval.

With my father, any lingering Quaker influence would have been unconscious; his family had ceased to be Quakers as early as the 1820s or 1830s, and, again, my father didn't often look back. But with my mother, the link with New England Puritanism was more conscious. It is curious in one sense that she did not identify with the other side of her family, her mother's family, the Gregorys—who *had* been southerners, in Tidewater Virginia, from the beginning, who had both the Tidewater accent and the southern propensity for fine living, who had by any measure been more socially prominent than the Tuttles. As a great aunt of mine on the Gregory side, in her cups, once lamented to me concerning the marriage back in 1901 of the well-born Jane Gregory to my football-playing grandfather Robert Tuttle, "Then poor Janie had to go and marry that Methodist preacher." But that Methodist preacher, the *embodiment* of plain living and high thinking, was my mother's father, and she nearly worshipped him. He died ten years before I was born so I never knew him, but I have inherited his volumes of Browning and Tennyson and the other high-minded Victorians, and from his marginal notes in those books and from his diary I feel I have come to know him at least a little. I see, for example, in his diary entries for the summer of 1925, the period of the Scopes trial, that he was very much on the side of Scopes, Clarence Darrow, and evolution, not William Jennings Bryan and the Genesis account of creation.

This phenomenon of father-worship among southern daughters of the late nineteenth and early twentieth centuries was hardly unique with my mother, and I have often wondered how it came to be. Numerous are the memoirs and diaries I have seen of southern women who speak reverentially of their fathers, can see no flaws in them and, in many cases, never marry at all because no other man can ever be as worthy. Such thinking was not only southern, of course — it was Victorian, in a larger sense — but I think it was even more true of the American South than the rest of the United States. Did it, in the beginning, have something to do with the cult of the Lost Cause, the spirit that led to the United Daughters of the Confederacy — the worship of the Confederate dead and maimed? Did it have something to do with the paragon of virtue, nearly the demigod, that became the mythological Robert E. Lee — with whom a number of these southern daughters seemed to identify their own fathers? I'm not sure. In any case, my mother, far from belonging to the UDC and not remotely a Lost Cause adherent, always spoke of her own father in near worshipful terms. And, to a lesser extent, she saw her brother, my Uncle Bob — also a star athlete and writer who occupied the pulpits of North Carolina's leading Methodist churches — in the same way. The remarkable thing is that my father never seemed to mind it, never felt competitive. All the while he poked fun at her ancestor-worship, he may even in his own way have fed it.

And something approaching ancestor-worship it was: not only the nearly two centuries of Tuttles in New England but the story of the hegira that had brought a younger son, Andrew Hull Tuttle, down to the western piedmont of North Carolina in 1800, where he had married the daughter of a Scots-Irish farmer and remained on her father's broad and fertile acres. My mother never mentioned that Andrew Hull took not only a southern wife but also a dozen or so slaves (this I found when I uncovered his will) left him by his father-in-law—apparently putting aside his Puritan scruples about the peculiar institution, at about the same time his New England cousins were mounting an abolitionist crusade. Maybe that—to expiate the sins of the father—is why three of Andrew Hull Tuttle's grandsons, postbellum, became racially liberal ministers and a granddaughter spent thirty-two years as a missionary in China.

In any case, if my father was in charge of politics in our home, my mother presided over religion. The Sunday morning brand I experienced was little different from that practiced in hundreds of other Methodist churches around the South: Sunday school at 9:30 or 10, then into the sanctuary at 11 for the main service. Our family always sat in the fourth row on the left side of the sanctuary, and I remember the starched shirt and scratchy pants I had to wear and, in the hymnal rack in front of me, the means of cooling off, those paper fans generously supplied by local funeral homes in the South before air-conditioning. I recall being assaulted by an assortment of smells, wax and varnish, toothpaste and aftershave, musty hymnals. I remember in particular the scent given off by an old man in a pew near us, a smell I have never encountered since—not body odor or bad breath or the aroma of any number of man-made products such as hair tonic and aftershave but rather something, as I reconstruct it, like old rotting flesh, not so much a smell as a kind of miasma emanating from deep within his being.

I mentioned earlier the egalitarian nature of my town, and nowhere was that seen better than in church: doctors, lawyers, teachers, insurance salesmen, electricians, plumbers, house painters, janitors, and their families all were there, sitting in the same pews with each other. The head usher was the owner of the town pool hall, off limits to young Methodist boys on Saturday nights. Our ministers, almost always graduates of Duke divinity school, tended to be on the progressive side of the southern religious spectrum, but that is not to say that old-time religion was missing. The hymns from an old Methodist hymnal were the classics—"Rescue the Perishing," "Amazing Grace" (not yet launched on its amazing ride to being America's state hymn), "Alas and Did My Saviour Bleed," and "Blessed Assurance"—and the lyrics were rousing, sometimes nearly rapturous: "Blessed assurance, Jesus is mine / O what a foretaste of glory divine / Heir of salvation, purchase of God / Born of his spirit, washed in his blood." Even if you didn't take to all the rest of the service, you could certainly get into the spirit of the music.

Those hymns were used to best effect during spring revival week. We might have called it "spring services," to distinguish it from the Baptists, but it was approximately the same—except, of course, Baptists baptized and Methodists christened. And the sermons, with Methodist calm assurance and sweet reason rather than voice-raising fervor, were more restrained. No tongue-speaking or foot-washing or snake-handling here, or even mention of hell-fire. But, whatever the sales pitch, the intent was the same—closing the deal, the ultimate moment when a convert came down the aisle to the altar and, in sight of the hundred or so assembled, gave his or her life "to Christ" and vowed to lead a new life.

As revival week went on—the services began Sunday

night and went through Thursday—the suspense would build: Would Lon West and Walter Zachary, finally, *this* year, come forward at the altar call the last night? Mencken once said southern towns had lynchings because people were bored and needed excitement, and I think revivals filled the same need with a lot less physical damage. You really did wait all week to see what would happen—I got into the waiting too when I was nine or ten—and on that final night as the organist played and the congregation sang "Just As I Am" you started shifting your eyes back to look at Lon, the genial county clerk of court, and Walt, a hard-boiled lawyer, both of whom were present only because their wives were pillars of the church. You were looking to see if they would make that initial move, putting the hymnbook down, so they could then shuffle out to the aisle and down to the front. It never happened in my time there, but when I was in college I was told that one of them—I forget which—finally did march down the aisle for blessed assurance. I wish I could have been there.

In some respects, my mother got into this as much as anyone else: she was certainly among those wanting Lon and Walt to come to the front. It's just that she disapproved of the terms some applied to the whole process— "getting saved" and "born again." There was something in that, I think, that smacked too much of tent revivals and the sawdust trail—of evangelists such as Billy Graham, whose appeals to come to Christ she felt were always too emotional and simplistic. She had lived too much—as a child—in city parsonages, had absorbed too much of that refined Duke brand of Methodism (and the tastes of her half-Episcopalian mother), had later read too much Bonhoffer and C. S. Lewis and Frank Laubach (all of whom she tried to incorporate into her Sunday school teaching though I'm not sure with what success) and had spent too much time discussing theology with her sister Emily, a college English professor and something of a doubter.

In a region in which religion seemed, and seems, to be largely about personal salvation, my mother's religion was at least as much outer-directed—horizontal, as the theologians would say—as it was vertical. I'm sure she, like everyone else in the church, prayed for the souls of Lon West and Walt Zachary, but she seemed to spend even more time talking to God about racial justice in South Africa or the latest incursion along the India-Pakistani border. This international interest came largely from her aunt, Lelia Tuttle, whose long missionary stint as a history professor in China and whose sympathy for the Chinese underclasses had given my mother a fairly ecumenical perspective. Unlike most Bible Belt Christians, she certainly did not think you had to believe in Christ to achieve salvation. She had already arrived at what I came to call her Gandhi clause: "Gandhi was a much better Christian than most Christians," she maintained, and thus certainly would be allowed to rub celestial shoulders with the Tuttles and other sons and daughters of the Gospel. She herself was even a doubter on certain matters: she said she wasn't altogether sure about the Virgin Birth, but that it really didn't matter. Her theological liberalism, however, stopped at any questioning of the divinity of Christ. Her mind refused to push that far.

I guess it's pretty commonplace to speak of people living their religion, but it sure seemed to me as a child that my parents did. They gave not 10 percent but more like 15 or 20 percent to various causes, mainly the Methodist Church—particularly the foreign missions program—but also, as time went on (and I suppose this broadens some definitions of "religion"), to Common Cause, the Sierra Club and other environmental groups, pro–gun control organizations, and so forth. Such giving wasn't really that much of a sacrifice for them, since they cared virtually nothing about money for themselves and felt they and their children needed very little. They owned their house, they always had a car that ran well enough, they got all of their vegetables out of the garden (as well as their milk from my father's dairy-farmer brother, and meat from another farmer brother), they sent their children mainly to state-supported universities, they traveled as much as they wanted, and they thought excessive consumption was, quite simply, in bad taste. When, in the 1960s, they built a small cottage in the mountains so my father could get away on weekends from the telephone and the pressures of school business, my mother was wracked with guilt because they had built something they might not have absolutely *needed*. To absolve herself, she threw the cottage doors open to any number of church groups who might use it for a retreat.

In some respects for her, as much as for my father, it finally came down to politics. Curiously, she would have agreed with Jerry Falwell (as well as with Falwell's opposite, Martin Luther King) in one important particular: religion had to be brought out of the church into the realm of political action, although she took her religion in a quite different direction than Falwell. Her feelings about politics, in fact, were even stronger—at least, they were expressed with more fervor—than my father's. Whenever Jesse Helms appeared on television, she wrinkled up her face and sputtered, "That *skunk!*"—or, if she felt ol' Jesse had done something particularly underhanded, "that *snake!*" When, in the 1980s, the Moral Majority reigned, she called it the *Immoral* Majority. And once, when Falwell or Pat Robertson or some other television Savonarola suggested, in effect, that it was impossible to be both a Democrat and a Christian, she answered back, "It's impossible to be a *Republican* and a Christian." What she had in mind was the social gospel, helping the poor and hungry and abandoned, areas she thought Falwell and Robertson were a little deficient in—but even to my father's way of thinking she may have gone a little far. She herself later relented, conceding that she might have been a little excessive, reasoning that, like good Hindus in India, some Republicans might get to heaven anyway—through what might be called the domestic equivalent of her Gandhi clause.

If my mother seems in many ways progressive for her time and place—more than a liberal Democrat, she really was a One-Worlder who trusted the United Nations more than the United States and believed there were few higher callings than trick-or-treating for UNICEF—she was in other ways profoundly conservative, you might even say provincial, and never more so than on the subject of alcohol. She detested the stuff, never tasted a drop, never allowed it in our home. Just why she objected so strongly, even more strongly than most small-town Methodists, I'm not sure. Certainly the Methodist Book of Discipline prohibited it, and her father and brother and a number of cousins were Methodist ministers, but I don't think that would have accounted for the fervor of her objections. Maybe it had something to do with her Grandfather Gregory, a socially prominent lawyer in the late nineteenth century who—at least she'd heard it rumored—had drunk heavily and may not have been the best of husbands.

In any case, there it was: no alcohol in our house. My father, who did not have the same scruples against Demon Rum, probably took a drink or two in his life, but, in Yadkinville, he went along with home rule—except for a bottle of rum he kept hidden in the closet and, without her knowing it, poured on the fruit cake every Christmas. "Don't you like the taste of that fruit cake?" he'd ask his children, and she never knew why we all roared. Sitting at the table, eating her fruit cake and violating the Methodist abstinence pledge, she never had a clue.

My friends in college, particularly northern friends, who visited me at home on occasion, could never quite figure out my parents—well-educated, well-traveled Adlai Stevenson Democrats, strong on civil rights, internationalists in foreign affairs, who nonetheless never touched a drop of alcohol, didn't allow it in their home, and joined with the fundamentalists to vote dry on every county alcohol referendum. Added to the paradox—this was in the late '60s when liberal Democrats weren't supposed to do such things—my father flew his flag every Fourth of July. My parents were, in some sense, I think, anachronisms. After all, in the late nineteenth century, prohibition had been a *progressive* cause, going hand in hand with civil rights and women's suffrage—and I think my parents inherited that set of assumptions. In fact, for a certain kind of North Carolinian of their generation and just before, they weren't that unusual at all; what else was Frank Graham, my father's mentor and hero, but a teetotaler and the most courageous southern political liberal of his generation—a plain liver and a high thinker.

Psychologists, of course, often hold forth on the sad fates of children who are the products of unhappy marriages, but I don't think I've ever seen a practitioner who writes on the perils of happy ones. There are hazards there too—mainly, that children grow up with such an ideal of marriage that they are spoiled, that they think their own marriages should be that good and are sorely disappointed when they fail to be. Such has probably been the case with me. But, all in all, I'm glad I grew up with the parents I had—and even, in most respects, grew up where I did. Which is to say, this is not one of those accounts of a provincial southern childhood in which the author celebrates, more than anything else, his or her escape from the clutches of ecclesiastical ignorance, racial bigotry, and general benightedness. The Methodist Church, through its summer assembly in the North Carolina mountains, let me have my first experience with racial integration, and that assembly, at Lake Junaluska, also taught a kind of religious tolerance rare in the South for its time. I think, if anything, I came to idealize Roman

Catholics—assumed, through my parents and through Catholics I had met at Lake Junaluska, that all of them were like the Kennedys, well educated, charming, liberal, articulate. (I'd barely been to northern cities, and had no idea that there might reside Catholics who bore their own share of racism and prejudice.) And I idealized Jews: Abraham Ribicoff, Sandy Koufax, and Lennie Rosenbluth were all I knew, and my mother threw in Einstein and Isaac Stern and Artur Rubenstein. You couldn't do any better than that.

Mainly, I think I emerged from my family and the Methodist Church—and even from the North Carolina hills—with a view of the world not much less enlightened (other than in matters bibulous) than that of a contemporary from, say, New Canaan or Shaker Heights. Not that the Methodism altogether took—there was something about it, in the long run, that was too cheerful, too optimistic, too *happy*, for my temperament. And the Wesleyan theology was somewhat hard to swallow—it didn't seem to take determinism adequately into account. But it did provide a base, and though I haven't been in a Methodist church in years, I took, quite literally, some of it with me. To this day, I keep under the back seat of my car an old Methodist hymnal, and when I'm on a long trip, alone, and getting sleepy, there's nothing that wakes me up better than reaching for the hymnal, opening the windows, and belting out a verse of "Rescue the Perishing."

4

My Magic Season

So there was the Church of Methodism and there was the Church of the Democratic Party, but most of all, when I was ten or twelve years old, growing up in the hills of North Carolina, there was—to borrow from Susan Sarandon in *Bull Durham*—the Church of ACC Basketball. And about this time, the mid-1950s, the Holy See of that church, its Rome, its Canterbury—hitherto the House that Case Built, in Raleigh—was about to shift twenty-five miles west to Chapel Hill. Not quite yet: the N.C. State Wolfpack, with Shavlik, Molodet, Maglio, and DiNardo—more exotic names to a southern schoolboy's ears—had won the ACC tournament in 1954, 1955, and 1956, as well as (just before the ACC came into being) six of the last seven Southern Conference tournament titles. But the Tar Heels, featuring the five New Yorkers Frank McGuire had brought to Chapel Hill, had tied Case's Wolfpack for the ACC's 1955–1956 regular season title and had virtually everyone back for the 1956–1957 season. There was the feeling that something big might be just ahead, but no one had any idea just how big.

It came at just the right time for me. My Carolina allegiance, growing gradually from the time McGuire had come to Chapel Hill in 1952, had become a near obsession by 1954. It was that year, at age eleven, that I had begun to play all the Carolina games in advance on my backyard court, and that year I had also written McGuire a long letter, expressing my undying devotion to the Tar Heels and asking for an autographed picture of the 1954–1955 team. He'd written back a personal letter, concluding with words I'm sure he dispensed to all aspiring Tar Heels who wrote him, but to my eleven-year-old eyes they were meant for me alone: "And if you continue to practice hard and work hard on your studies and listen to your parents, I'm sure when you're ready for college you'll be plenty good enough to play for Carolina."

And with the letter had come the autographed picture, featuring Lennie Rosenbluth, then a sophomore, who had already replaced Charlie Justice as my all-time Carolina sports hero. Ah, the contrast: Justice, not only the All-American but the All-American boy, from the North Carolina mountains, open-faced, always smiling—as opposed to Rosenbluth, tall and slender, the dark, mysterious Semitic prince, the brooding presence from the Bronx. After his sophomore year Rosenbluth was listed on the roster as being not from the Bronx but from Greeneville, Tennessee, but I couldn't come to terms with the move. I went to the T volume of my encyclopedia and located Greeneville on a map. It was a small town in the mountains. Why, I wondered even then, would a Jew from the Bronx move to a small, probably backward, mountain town? Why had Mr. Rosenbluth, whoever he was, pulled up stakes and taken Lennie with him? I didn't know much in those days, but I did know, from my college basketball education, a little something about ethnicity, and there couldn't have been many Jews, if any, in the Tennessee hills. I could picture the tall, brooding Lennie walking down the streets of Greeneville, in the midst of all those ruddy-faced Anglo-Saxons. (I didn't know what they were called then, but I knew what they looked like.) I still saw Lennie as being from the Bronx, and when, on my backyard court, I announced the Carolina starting lineup, I stuck with the Bronx. It rolled off the tongue better.

In the picture Coach McGuire sent, Rosenbluth stood out, but I also found, above their autographs, the other New Yorkers, Vayda and Radovich, as well as various other out-of-staters, there not being (Wake Forest's Dickie Hemric aside) a lot of great native North Carolina basketball players in those days. *White* basketball players, that is: there was at about that time, or just afterward, Walt Bellamy from New Bern, Lou Hudson from Greensboro, and Happy Hairston from Winston-Salem, but they — being African American in the Jim Crow South — were destined to end up in the Big Ten, not the ACC.

The picture of the '54–55 team went immediately on my bedroom wall, where it would remain until I went off to college seven years later. I still know the entire roster, down to the twelfth man, Tuffy Henderson — who never played a minute all year as far as I know, but if I met him today, I could tell him not only his hometown but his height and weight when he was nineteen, back in 1954. I knew and still know the heights and weights and hometowns of all the '54–'55 Heels. *And still know:* that is the remarkable thing. At a time when I have long since forgotten the names of minor Elizabethan dramatists, seventeenth-century metaphysical poets, and the exact order of the U.S. presidents between Grant and Mc-Kinley—all learned later and with some professional goal in mind—I can still come up with such minutiae off 1950s basketball rosters.

But the 1954–1955 team, in fact, was still mediocre. It was only in the 1955–1956 season, when the four New York Irishmen—Kearns, Brennan, Quigg, and Cunningham—became sophomores and thus eligible for the varsity, that Carolina became good; and only in 1956–1957, with the four Irishmen teaming with the senior Rosenbluth, that the Heels became truly great. Never was the Church of Basketball to witness more miracles than during that 1956–1957 season, a season miraculous not only from my provincial point of view but also in the eyes of those with more of a national vision. Carolina's '56–'57 season was to be, arguably, a college basketball team's greatest season ever, culminated by the contest Frank Deford has called the greatest single college game ever played.

I was in need of a good season. That fall, 1956, I had experienced a double humiliation. Not only had Eisenhower beaten Stevenson again—and, along the way, I'd run into double-teams, had my Stevenson badges ripped off and "I Like Ike" bumper stickers put on my notebooks—but Carolina had gone through a 2–8 football season, and those two victories later had to be forfeited. That month too, only a few weeks before Ike's landslide victory, the hated Yankees had beaten my Dodgers in a seven-game World Series; Don Newcombe had choked again.

And my own athletic prowess was being called into question—largely because, even more than before, I was falling behind my friends in height. In football I had also lost some of my speed and no longer played halfback in sandlot games; the only thing I could do well was catch passes. In baseball, in center field, I was labeled good field, no hit. And, most of all, in basketball I seemed to be in decline. Bones McKinney's predicted state of basketball nirvana, big-man height and little-man skills, had not arrived. Long gone were those glory days of vertical leaping in Durham, or even of being the best player in my class in Yadkinville. I was now no better than third best. On my eighth-grade team I was the primary ballhandler and passer, but assist men got no respect in those days. I remember only one highlight from that entire year—stealing the ball and driving for the winning basket against a team from the other side of the county. Otherwise, all was forgettable.

So I needed the Heels to be not just good but great in the winter of 1956–1957. I remember reading McGuire's preseason prediction that the record would probably be about the same as the previous year, 18–6. Still, the Heels were ranked number four nationally preseason, so I decided to keep a basketball diary for the season. The early results were unremarkable: in their first game Carolina beat a mediocre semi-pro team by the unimpressive score of 84–70 (the same night, I read in the paper, that number one Kansas had won much more impressively, with

7'1" super-sophomore Wilt Chamberlain pouring in 52 in his debut), and then routinely dispensed with subpar foes Furman and Clemson and George Washington. In the fifth game, playing at South Carolina, in what was later to become a pattern, the Heels squeaked out an overtime win. Then, after a home win against Maryland, they went on the road for nearly a month, first beating a good NYU team in Madison Square Garden, then winning a tournament in Boston, and finally returning to Raleigh for the greatest holiday tournament in the country, the Dixie Classic, an event, played on N.C. State's home court, that State had dominated since its inception in 1949. Carolina had never won it, had never even come close.

The Dixie Classic was not only important to the Heels, it was also perhaps the great occasion of my youth—for this was about the only time, every year from 1954 to 1959, that I actually got to see Carolina and State, Duke and Wake Forest play in person, as well as four visiting teams who were always among the nation's best. The greatest field ever would be in 1958 when number one Cincinnati, with the nation's top scorer, Oscar Robertson, as well as three other teams in the nation's top six—and another team that later reached the national semifinals— were all in the tournament. (Previously undefeated Cincinnati and the Big O would lose twice, both to State and Carolina, before slinking back to the banks of the Ohio.) But the 1956 field—Iowa, Utah, DePaul, and West Virginia with Hot Rod Hundley, along with North Carolina's Big Four—was no slouch either.

The Dixie Classic, usually played the last Thursday, Friday, and Saturday of December, was always my main

Christmas gift. On Christmas morning my sisters would find two chairs beside the tree filled with clothes and records and books for them; I would find on my chair only the small book of tournament tickets and a box of chocolate-covered cherries, but that's all I wanted. Early the Thursday morning after Christmas my father and I would head out on the 130-mile trip to Raleigh where we would stay three days and see four games each day—that is, ten hours of basketball a day, or some thirty hours in all. We usually made the trip with one of my father's political allies, whose son, playing for another school in the county, was probably my biggest rival. He would continue in that role in high school and briefly in college, since he was to play on the Wake Forest freshman team during my own modest career with the Tar Babies. Later he would leave North Carolina, make a million in business at a young age, and become one of the "golfing buddies" that O. J. Simpson would mention by name in his famous "suicide note."

But at that point Jay and I cared only about the outcome of the Classic—since he, even then, was as fanatical a Deac as I was a Tar Heel. We could agree only in our mutual hatred of N.C. State, and we sang lustily out the back windows as we passed through Winston-Salem and Greensboro and Burlington (at least until our fathers shut us up), "Far away in Raleigh's ditches / There's a place we hate / Where ten thousand sons of bitches / Go to N.C. State." This year it looked like it would be different—one of us would win. Carolina was the highest-ranked team in the ACC, and Wake Forest was second. The Wolfpack, though playing the Classic at home as always, had lost both Shavlik and Molodet from the previous year's conference championship team, and was finally ready to be knocked off.

I was a veteran Dixie Classic–goer by this point — this was my third one — and my father and I had the routine down. In the morning of the second and third days we would go to the state museum of natural history or the state archives, or Dad would see some state school officials, and after an early lunch of barbecue (much better in these eastern regions than the hill–country stuff back home) we would head for Reynolds Coliseum, arriving just before the Star–Spangled Banner. Then the lights would go down and the spotlight would shine on the starting lineups, announced by the same C. A. Dillon, Jr., I imitated in my backyard games.

Our seats were usually near the top, and by the end of the second game of the afternoon, a haze of cigarette smoke would already be filling the coliseum and it would be hard to see the floor clearly. No one would have thought of prohibiting smoking in those days, certainly not in the Tar Heel State. If Reynolds was the House that Case Built, North Carolina was the State that Tobacco Built. Both Duke and Wake Forest were constructed on tobacco fortunes, and Carolina and State rested on tax revenues from tobacco companies. It showed everywhere. Not only were most of the 12,400 fans — mostly middle-age and older men — smoking, but Ray Reeve broadcast on the Tobacco Sports Network, and the territory in which the four schools were located was already becoming known as Tobacco Road.

After the afternoon basketball session and a supper

break at 5:30 or so—always the S&W cafeteria, always hamburger steak and french fries and chocolate milk (from which comes an unnatural affection for cafeterias to this day)—we came back for the night session. In between games, both afternoon and night, I went down to the floor and worked the entrances through which the players came on and off the courts. The autograph book I unearthed recently seems largely filled with names from the '56 Classic. I say largely since the first name in the book is Charlie Justice and the second Dickie Hemric, and those eminences obviously came from earlier times. But all the rest are '56 Blue Devils and Demon Deacons and Wolfpack and West Virginia Mountaineers (including the All–American Hundley), and most of all Tar Heels—Rosenbluth, Bob Cunningham, Danny Lotz and, particularly, "To Fred, Good luck, Frank McGuire." I find I even have the autograph of the Dixie Classic Queen, one Marie Barlow, who at this moment must be in her late sixties but in my mind is still as gorgeous as she was in that picture in the Classic program in December 1956.

The '56 Classic games went exactly as I would have played them in the backyard. The first day Carolina, Duke, State, and Wake Forest all beat the visitors; the second day Carolina beat Duke, and in the finals Saturday night Carolina beat Wake 63–55 for their first Classic title. (West Virginia, with the highly touted Hundley, lost all three of its games, often the fate of highly ranked teams who ventured onto Tobacco Road.) The Heels had now won eleven in a row and had risen to number two in the country. My father and I filed out of Reynolds Coliseum about midnight, got in our car, and headed west through the middle of the night, past Durham and Greensboro and Winston-Salem, away from the lowlands where high-intensity basketball and barbecue flourished and into the hills toward home.

When we got there—and after a short night's sleep—I got up, read the sports section, and then reflected in my diary on the Heels' fortunes. And I see now I jotted one other thing in the diary—an entry based on a news story I had just read, about Mississippi State pulling out of another holiday tournament in Evansville, Indiana, because their opponent, the Evansville Aces, had black players. That's all I wrote, just the fact, no commentary. And I'm not sure why I included even that. The diary contains little else of sociological interest, and despite reading about the Emmett Till lynching in Mississippi a year or two before, I was not particularly focused on race in those days. Maybe it was just a smug show of what I thought to be Upper South superiority to Deepest Dixie. I had just come from a segregated coliseum, and none of the North Carolina teams had any black players on them—but, I may have reasoned, at least we didn't mind playing *against* black players.

The easy part, the undramatic part, of the season was over for the Tar Heels—so far, only one overtime victory that lent itself to high drama, the rest relatively easy wins. But what was to come over the next three months would be the stuff of basketball legend. It began with a game that was tougher than it should have been, an on-the-road, come-from-behind victory over an outmanned but fired-up William & Mary team. Then came easy home wins against Clemson (what else: the Heels, to this day, have never lost to the Tigers at home—an NCAA–record fifty–one straight wins) and Virginia, and a trip to N.C. State to take on the recently defanged Wolfpack. This one I remember well. The Heels won 85–57 in Raleigh on a snowy Tuesday night—at least snowy in western North Carolina where I heard the game—and, since Kansas had just been defeated, Carolina rose to number one in the country. Psychologically, it was huge. Not only were the Heels number one for the first time in history but also their ancient foe had been not just beaten but demolished, and right there in the Pack's den. After the game I went out with my father to check the condition of the county roads, and he found them too icy for school the next day. As he called WSJS in Winston-Salem to report the school closing, I remember what I was thinking: the Heels have won fifteen in a row and are number one, Rosenbluth is averaging nearly thirty points a game, school is called off for tomorrow, and in the kitchen are a pan of cinnamon buns and a dish of snowcream waiting for me. Life was as perfect as it could get.

Then the really tight times began. At semester break—just after the State game—Carolina lost its top two reserves, Tony Radovich, whose eligibility had expired, and Billy Hathaway, a 6'11" center who hadn't made his grades. It was down to the starting five, and they were headed on the road for most of the rest of the season. The winning streak continued at Western Carolina, but almost came to an end at Maryland. The Terps led by four with two minutes to go, and Rosenbluth fouled out thirty seconds later. The Heels came back and sent it into overtime, then double overtime, before they finally pulled it out. The other four starters had played the entire game without a rest.

The next game, against Duke in early February, was equally tense—the Devils leading by five at the half, and the Heels pulling out a 75–73 victory in the last seconds. Playing next at Virginia, the Heels had to come from behind in the second half to beat the woeful (3–14) Cavaliers. Next, in their second game of the season against Wake Forest, with Rosenbluth having fouled out with three minutes to play, the Heels barely won 72–69. After an easy win over State in Chapel Hill, the Heels had to come from six points down in the second half to beat South Carolina a second time. I had seen none of these games—none was televised—and listening on the radio is the most painful way there is to keep up with a game. I've known play-by-play men—one, in fact, who has gained great renown—who call it for their own team: that is, they first call it the way they want to see it—"Mullen drives, shoots, it's *good!*"—and then mention almost as an afterthought that the goal was wiped out by a charging foul. You can't trust 'em. Even good stuff might not be good after all.

But for all those games since the Dixie Classic I'd had to depend on the radio, until, in mid-February, the Heels came to Winston-Salem, again to play Wake Forest, who—despite their two previous losses to the Heels—had lost to almost no one else and were still a ranked team. By this point in my career as a basketball fan I had almost stopped playing and announcing all the Carolina games in advance on my backyard court: I had my own elementary school team to play on, and besides I had come to realize how ridiculous it all must have looked to the neighbors. But for the Wake game I again took to the backyard. The fantasy game, in classic schoolboy fashion, went down to the wire and the Heels won by one.

The actual game, which I saw in Winston–Salem the next night, was almost as tight. Wake led by eight in the second half, and by one with forty-five seconds left — at which point Rosenbluth was fouled and, with the home crowd making as much noise as possible, hit both shots. The Heels won. After the game the Deacs' Bones McKinney, already known as the Clown Prince of Basketball for his sidelines antics (he'd once seatbelted himself into his chair to keep from getting a technical), was deadly serious for once. Carolina, he implied, was lucky, and — echoing Everett Case from a couple of weeks earlier — if they kept playing this close to the edge, soon it was going to catch up with them.

In fact, Bones said, it would catch up with them in their next game, against Duke in Durham. It almost did. The Devils led with under four minutes to go, but then Rosenbluth took over and ended up with forty points. That concluded a perfect regular season, twenty-four in a row, but the real pressure began now. Throughout February McGuire had kept saying he himself wished the Heels would lose in order to relieve some of the tension before the ACC tournament. In those days, even if you were number one in the country (which the Heels still were), if you lost in the ACC tourney, your season was over: no NCAAs, no chance for the national title. An easy first–round win, in which Rosenbluth scored forty-five, set up the agonizing test — having to beat a superb Wake Forest team for the fourth time in one season.

The game was on television, and I remember what it came down to: Wake leading 59–58 with less than a minute and Carolina with the ball — exactly the same situation as in Winston-Salem three weeks earlier. Everyone knew the ball would go to Rosenbluth, and it did, just to the left of the lane. Bottled up on every side, he swept toward the top of the lane and, right at the foul line, threw up what looked like an impossible hook shot — "a Globetrotter shot," McGuire called it after the game — as he was being fouled. It swished. After he hit the free throw for a two-point lead, Carolina held on to win 61–59. As *Raleigh News and Observer* columnist Dick Herbert wrote the next day, "How much longer can it go on? How much more can the heart stand?" My heart was fine, but everything else was suffering. My father said I wasn't thinking about anything but basketball, wasn't reading anything but the sports page. It was now mid-March and he'd begun getting his garden ready for planting. He conscripted me as always, but now I kept slipping away, running up to the backyard court to shoot baskets.

The win over Wake Forest in the semi-finals was the real ACC championship game: the twenty-point rout of South Carolina in the finals was anticlimactic. The Heels' first-round Eastern Regional win in Madison Square Garden brought only a minor scare. Sure, Yale had led with less than seven minutes to go, but that was getting to be routine. Wins over Canisius and Syracuse in the Eastern semifinals and finals were pretty decisive too, and with the Syracuse win, their thirtieth straight, the Heels broke the NCAA record for most consecutive wins in a season. I'd had to hear both games on the radio. They had been televised, I later learned, in the Raleigh–Chapel Hill area, but not in the remote vastness of Carolina's western piedmont.

Basketball playoffs are like election night: returns roll in from across the country, and the returns that Saturday night told me that, while Carolina was winning the East, Michigan State was winning in what was called the Mideast, Kansas in the Midwest, and—a few hours later— San Francisco in the West. It would be, said the pundits, the finest Final Four field ever, although they didn't use precisely that term—"Final Four," now a part of the nation's alliterative consciousness, being a term that did not come in until the '60s. In any case, the teams that would meet in Kansas City that weekend in late March for the national championship were loaded: number-one-ranked Carolina; number two Kansas with Wilt Chamberlain, already being called the most dominant athlete ever to play college basketball; the two-time defending national champion San Francisco Dons, with an all-time record of 11–0 in NCAA play; and a Michigan State team that had come on extremely strong the last six weeks of the season and was a dark horse to win the whole thing.

What the Heels were to experience in Kansas City that weekend was unprecedented in college basketball, and no team has experienced anything like it in the nearly fifty years since. First, they had to go through Michigan State to get to Kansas, and going through Michigan State meant going through Jumpin' Johnny Green, a sophomore leaper who, it was said and I believed it, could take a dime off the top of the backboard. Previously that year Carolina had endured overtime and double-overtime games. Now they faced a triple-overtime game, and what Bones had earlier said was true—they were lucky—but they were also awfully good. Michigan State seemed to have the game wrapped up near the end of the second overtime. With eleven seconds left the Spartans led 64–62 and had Johnny Green on the line. All Green had to do—in those days before the three-point shot—was to make one free throw and it was all over. He missed, and the Heels' junior forward Pete Brennan grabbed the rebound, took the ball the length of the court and hit a twelve-foot jumper just before the buzzer. As Rosenbluth later said, "I knew we had it won after that," and they did, in the third overtime, even with three of their starters having fouled out.

That game I did see on television, and I can still replay Brennan's full-court drive and shot in my mind's eye. It is to that moment, or at least to that game, that I think I can trace my intimacy with the television set in a tight game, the visceral feeling I have (along with a couple of hundred thousand others out there, to be sure) that I can determine the outcome of a game by the manner in which I watch it. As a friend and former student of mine would later write in *Sports Illustrated* of me and my conduct—the only time to my knowledge I have ever been cited in that august journal—he "believes he can control games by maintaining the same posture throughout the contest and by doing some kind of weird voodoo gesture with his fingers every time an opposing player shoots a free throw." Not absolutely correct—I wouldn't call them voodoo gestures—but very close. That night against Michigan State I selected my place, on the couch just to the left of my father's chair, and I don't remember moving until Brennan hit his shot. As for the free-throw gesture, the first time I ever applied it was against Johnny Green. And it worked.

The next day, a Saturday—the day of the Kansas game—I seem to remember as I remember no other day of my young life. Not only the game itself, but everything about the day. In the morning I shot basketball in the backyard, but for some reason decided not to play the game in advance—perhaps the first sign of the superstitious fan I much later was to become. In the afternoon I drove out with my father to my uncle's farm, and in the early evening I went with him by the church where he had some things to take care of. For supper we had steak and french fries—a rare occurrence in my home, saved for special Saturday nights—but after supper I still had a long time to go before the game would begin. I had done all my reading about the game: though Carolina was number one and Kansas number two, the Jayhawks were favored. They *should* have been favored. They had routed defending national champion San Francisco, 80–56, in their semifinal game. They were also playing what was essentially a home game, just over forty miles from Lawrence. And they had Wilt, hailed as the greatest college player ever. The David vs. Goliath script was already written.

The game itself didn't get under way until almost 10:30 Eastern time, and no one was very optimistic. My father sat in his brown leather chair, settling back stoically, prepared to take whatever came, just like the Jayhawks were the GOP and what lay ahead would be just another Democratic defeat at the polls. I sat at the same place as the night before, on the couch, and my mother in her chair on my father's other side, not really caring about basketball but aware that this was an event of great magnitude, like Queen Elizabeth's coronation or the Democratic convention, and her presence was required. My sisters, one somewhat more interested than the other, flitted in and out of the room, pretending concern, saying, much to my annoyance, "How's it *going?*"

In fact, it was going very well at first. McGuire stuck to the David and Goliath script perfectly by having Carolina's shortest player, 5'11" Tommy Kearns, jump center against the 7'1" Chamberlain. There was a strategic reason—Chamberlain was going to get the tip no matter whom he jumped against, and the Heels would have four tall players to go after the ball this way—but it was also a psychological ploy, turning the contest into a sort of spectacle and throwing Kansas off its game. It worked: the Heels, holding the ball each time until they got just the shot they wanted, jumped to a 19–7 lead. But then the Jayhawks—who would have been a very good team even without Wilt—began their comeback, inspired by a boisterous crowd. They went ahead in the second half, and all looked bleak for the Heels when Rosenbluth fouled out with 1:45 to go. (For nearly fifty years I had remembered it was exactly 1:45, and when I saw the game recently on tape there it was—1:45 on the dot.) That was the most dejected I had been all year, even more than the night before with Johnny Green on the line. But Kearns and Cunningham led an unlikely rally against the Jayhawks and a hostile crowd that tied the game at 46 at the end of regulation.

Again—just like the night before—one overtime, then two, then three. With six seconds left in the third overtime and the Heels down by one—a time they would have looked for Rosenbluth if he'd been there—center Joe Quigg was fouled making a move down the lane. Quigg was the Carolina player I trusted least in the clutch, but McGuire was again the master psychologist. In the timeout just before Quigg's shots—in words that would become a part of Carolina legend—he said, *"When you make the shots, Joe, drop back fast and help out on Chamberlain."* It was foreordained. Joe made them both, sprinted to the other end of the court and batted away a pass intended for Wilt. Kearns, who had begun the game jumping against Wilt, ended it by throwing the ball toward the rafters of Kansas City's Municipal Auditorium, and when the ball came down the Heels were 32–0 and national champions.

I reacted as I had the night before, and as, I fear, I have on numerous such occasions in the nearly fifty years since—leaping up, flathanding the ceiling, punching the air. "Calm down, Son," my father said, and you could not tell from his face whether it had been victory or defeat. But it had been a monumental victory, *still* the greatest in Carolina history—greater than the '82 national championship win over Georgetown, decided by Michael Jordan's jumper with seventeen seconds left; greater than the down-to-the-wire title game eleven years later against Michigan; greater than the eight-points-in-seventeen-seconds comeback win over Duke in 1974. It was the greatest because it was the birth of the Carolina legend, the game that would launch the Heels toward their position as the winningest program in college basketball over the next four decades. I didn't have to wait for Frank Deford and others, years later, to pronounce it not only Carolina's but college basketball's greatest game. (Not greatest in quality of play — Duke-Kentucky in 1992 or Carolina-Georgetown in 1982 come closer to that — nor in the transcendent majesty of the players, but greatest in sheer drama, endurance, and suspense.) I knew it at the time. It was well after midnight but I went out to my backyard court and reshot Quigg's free throws in the moonlight, my self-made crowd noise roaring in my ears. They were good.

That game I later took with me wherever I went, and fifteen years later, in my first teaching job at the University of Alabama, I met a new colleague, exactly my age, who as an eighth-grader on the plains of Kansas had not only seen that same game on television but also had the same emotional investment in it that I had. Only he had been for the other team. When the game was over, he later wrote me, "I knew I'd watched something seismic, something I would simply never forget." Nearly fifty years later Ralph Voss still writes and e-mails me about the game, on one recent occasion saying that he still dreams about it, on another sending me the box score and lamenting that the Jayhawks couldn't hit their foul shots. "I'll never get over '57," he wrote just last year. "Being from Kansas I can bleed, and I can't even wrap about me that tragic shawl of loss that is uniquely the

South's." Wilt Chamberlain wasn't quite as poetic, but the loss caused him to stay away from Kansas for forty years, and when he returned less than two years before his death, this toughened veteran of 1,045 NBA games and six championship series told a packed Allen Field House crowd that the Carolina defeat was "the toughest loss of my life . . . It was devastating because I felt I had let KU down."

Wilt's was heartfelt, but I find Ralph Voss's lament even more moving. As I think about him watching the game in a late-winter blizzard, across from a wheat field in his house on the outskirts of Lyons, Kansas (population forty-five hundred then, thirty-five hundred now), I'm always aware that the loser—a southerner after all, used to it—could as easily have been, *should* have been, me. Voss too had a goal nailed up in his backyard, he knew the entire Kansas roster as I knew the Carolina one. He wanted to be Maurice King and Ron Loneski as much as I wanted to be Rosenbluth and Brennan. (*No* one could be Wilt.) And he wanted that final game just as much as I did.

The words "miracle" and "God" are altogether misappropriated in talking about sport—if there is a God, that deity is on neither side—but when I was thirteen and newly triumphant, it's easy to see why I believed in both. As several basketball sages, now with perspective, have observed, the '57 Carolina season was the *nearest thing* to a miracle season you can find. You can find other individual games that come closer, but not an entire season. As Frank McGuire kept saying that year, "Basketball is not an undefeated sport." There have been rare exceptions—

San Francisco in 1955 and 1956, UCLA in 1967, 1972, and 1973, Indiana in 1976 (and no one since then) — but in those cases there was a reason. Those teams — San Francisco with Bill Russell and K. C. Jones, UCLA with Lew Alcindor and then Bill Walton, Indiana with all the ingredients — were simply so much better than everyone else.

But Carolina in '57 was not. They were not at all a dominant team, and they played twenty-four of their thirty-two games on the road. They *should* have lost to Kansas. They probably should have lost to Michigan State. They should have lost to Maryland in College Park. They should have lost at least once to Wake Forest. Eight times that season, almost always away from home, they trailed or were tied within the last two minutes of the game, and four times — always on the road — they went into overtime. They played a total of nine overtimes in all (counting the three each against Michigan State and Kansas), each one potentially a sudden death, and they either survived or won them all — often with their only true star, Rosenbluth, having fouled out, usually with the other four starters having gone all the way with no rest. In the finals against Kansas, all the starters except Rosenbluth played the entire fifty-five minutes (on top of having also played three overtimes the night before), and Quigg played the last thirty, guarding Chamberlain, with four fouls. Similar improbabilities happened in other Carolina games in 1957. In truth, the Heels could have lost nine or ten games that season. But they lost none. So, as well as feeling awe at the poise of the Tar Heel starters and the coaching genius of Frank McGuire, it would have been easy for a thirteen-year-old kid to think God wore Carolina blue that season.

And was on *my* side—not just McGuire's and Rosenbluth's but mine. That's the way really committed sports fans, especially young ones, take it—altogether personally. For at least two or three years after '57, if I was in a game and the score was close and I was anywhere near my opponent in ability, I was certain I would win, because I—OK, Carolina—had been there before and had come through in '57. (Did Voss, out in Kansas, also see the world differently after '57? I never asked.) That's the way it is with people who play games. I remember a distinctly average quarterback who led Alabama to a national championship in 1980. He didn't have much of an arm, he wasn't particularly fast, but he was convinced that God's plan included a national title for the Crimson Tide. The fact that God's plan didn't is irrelevant. He'd always come through on third and long.

As for me, natural law crept in soon enough, and the old certainty eventually wore off. But not my feeling about the 1957 team—a team, I am ashamed to confess, that I was more committed to than any team I was ever to play on. (And *there* is the curious thing: fans, in some weird way, seem to care more than the players.) When, in 2004, the '57 team returned to Chapel Hill's Smith Center to be recognized at halftime—Rosenbluth a retired high school teacher and coach in Florida, Kearns a stockbroker, Brennan a businessman, Quigg a dentist—I was amazed at the depth of my response. They were all old men now, but I still saw Rosenbluth, the dark prince, swishing the impossible hook from the foul line against Wake Forest,

Brennan hitting the clutch jumper against Michigan State to keep the season alive. In an earlier newspaper interview Rosenbluth said that most of his high school students and players did not even know he had been an All-American, the national player of the year on a national championship team—all that was in the past. That astounded me. Not know Rosenbluth? Impossible. At age eleven and twelve and thirteen that's all I did know, back in that season when every game *did* come out just as they'd always come out on my backyard court, in that age of limitless belief, that land of unchecked possibility.

5

Hornet

In the ninth grade, and then the tenth, Bones Mc-Kinney's prediction still hadn't panned out. I was still short—5'6" during my freshman year, 5'9" as a sophomore—and was consigned again to the backcourt, where I was considered a good shot and a decent, though hardly dazzling, ball-handler. It didn't matter much those two years anyway. Our high school was so small—only three hundred students or so for the four grades—that sophomores, or even freshmen if they were reasonably good, made the varsity. But, unless they were very good, or very big, they didn't play much.

I was neither big nor very good except at outside shooting, and thus I spent the first half of my freshman year sitting on the varsity bench except when the other team went into a zone. At that point the coach—a biology teacher who reversed the usual high school stereotype in that he was a very good teacher and a very poor coach—called on me to jack 'em up from outside and bring 'em out of the zone. Thus developed my first nickname, "Zonebuster." At least Coach Johnson called on me until a particular game against a close rival, in which I was summoned into action with the score tied, the clock winding down, and the crowd going wild. I shot an air ball. After that—indignity of indignities for a once hot-shot freshmen, even one 5'6"—I was sent down to the junior varsity, where I remained for a good part of the rest of the season.

I was part of a freshman class that was supposed to bring the Yadkinville Hornets back to basketball glory—which they indeed had once enjoyed—by our junior or senior year. No longer considered the best player in the class, I had been eclipsed by Johnny Crater, already 6'4" and 200 pounds and starting for the varsity. Also making the varsity was Michael Adams, a good all-around athlete who was also now a six-footer. Both were veterans of my backyard games, and had spent their share of time plunging into the lumber pile. Jimmy Dobbins—5'9" in the seventh grade, 5'9" in the ninth, still to be 5'9" as a senior and for eternity—hadn't made the basketball varsity, but that fall he had distinguished himself on the gridiron and was seen as a hoopster for the future.

I said our school was small and so it was, and so were the other five high schools in the county. But the quality of basketball was remarkably high for such a backwater. Dickie Hemric, the Wake Forest All-American who had set all sorts of scoring and rebounding records and had gone on to play for the Boston Celtics, came from Jonesville, a town on the other side of the county, and he had taken his team to great heights in high school as well. Although Boonville (named, as was much else around me, for Daniel Boone, who had been born not far away) and

East Bend were also consistent powers, Jonesville meant basketball royalty in our county and in the region in general. Their coach, John Mathis, was the John Wooden, later the Dean Smith, of hoops in our area. A gentleman, always poised, well dressed, and well spoken, he was also a disciplined, demanding taskmaster. And he won, year after year, turning out a number of college players in the process.

Because of Coach Mathis, because of Jonesville's eye-catching blue uniforms (ours were blue too but lacked something), and because their cheerleaders were prettier and classier than any other cheerleaders, Jonesville always seemed a cut above the rest of the county. The way they held themselves when they entered the gym in street clothes—at about halftime of the girls' game—the way they took the court for warm-ups, the way they ran drills, the confidence they had in close games: all seemed to make them better than the rest of us. The term *dynasty* in the 1950s and then 1960s came to mean the Celtics or UCLA; to me, before that, it meant Jonesville. And not just the team but, I thought in those days, the town of Jonesville as well. Later, when I got away from Yadkin County and looked back, I realized that an outsider might have challenged that characterization: sociologically speaking, Jonesville was just another run-down appendage to an across-the-river mill town. But not to my eyes in 1957 and 1958.

And thus my only shining moment my freshman year was all the better because it came against Jonesville in the semifinals of the county tournament, played in our gym, with all thousand seats taken. I had returned from

the ignominy of the junior varsity a couple of weeks before—a move comparable, in baseball, to calling minor-
leaguers up to the majors at the end of the season—and
had hoped to get a lot of playing time against the Blue
Jays. In fact, I didn't get in until the fourth quarter, when
there was no zone left to bust and the game was virtually
out of reach. But once in, I hit four in a row from twenty
feet or so, what would now be three-point range. We still
lost, by ten or fifteen points, but I figured I had at least
redeemed myself from the midseason air ball that had got
me sent into junior varsity exile. Besides, as a member of
the boosters club told me as I came off the court, "It's all
about the future."

The future didn't come the next year when I was a
sophomore. Though I had grown to all of 5'9" I was still
in the backcourt, where jumping ability didn't do a lot of
good. Because we had a couple of upperclassmen guards
ahead of me, I didn't see much more action than in the
year before except, again, as a designated shooter. I even,
for a brief spell, was sent down again to the junior varsity, to "work on [my] total game." Which isn't to say,
however, that my sophomore year, or the one before,
hanging around the locker room, was a total waste, at
least not in terms of education—the kind you couldn't get
in Mrs. Buchanan's English or Mr. Shore's chemistry
class.

Prior to those two enlightening years, most of my
knowledge in matters of the flesh had come from a couple
of summer and weekend jobs I'd held and would continue to hold through high school, one as a painter on the
Yadkin County school maintenance crew, the other as a

bag boy in a grocery store. On the paint crew my primary mentors were two brothers in their thirties, Claude and Reuben Hardy, from Andy Griffith country, just across the river in Surry County. But even more important, in the ninth grade, had been Roland Taylor, the butcher at the Yadkin County Freezer Locker, so called because it had begun, back in the pre–home freezer days, as a place for people to store their beef and pork and then later had become a full-service grocery store.

Roland was about fifty, a short stout man with a round, ruddy, pockmarked face, looking somewhat (I later realized) like the Miller in Chaucer's *Canterbury Tales*. He took seriously his role as counselor and guide to two fourteen-year-old boys, Johnny Vestal and me, giving us advice on how to get deflowered and by whom. The whom, he said, was easy: it should be an older woman. He had in mind, in particular, the wife of a prominent local businessman, a stodgy and eminently respectable woman of about forty-five whose groceries I used to bag and carry. She had no apparent charms as far as I could see and no interest at all in breaking in young boys—in fact, she was a *much* "older woman." But who was I, I first thought, to question Roland?

When, finally, Johnny and I did challenge him, saying we'd like someone a little less seasoned, he took it well, and went on to counsel us more generally in matters of carnality. First he ventured into that treacherous intersection of sex and race. "Some will say," he pronounced gravely, looking over his white blood-splattered butcher's apron, "you can't knock a nigger woman up." I'd heard that too, but I'd wondered, seeing all the coffee-colored faces around, not so much in Yadkin County but certainly in Winston. "But you *can*," he affirmed, "so be careful." He then went on to address getting laid in broader terms, maintaining that it was a mighty serious matter: "It takes five drops of your best blood," he said, looking first at Johnny and then me. And then, with some urgency—as if I, barely pubescent, was intent upon it that very night—"Don't ride 'em bareback." "Yessir," I looked Roland in the eye. "I won't ride 'em bareback."

After studying with Roland, I was ready for the locker room; and what astounds me now, looking back, is how little, in certain regards, those connoisseurs of the flesh—usually juniors and seniors who were veterans of hot, steamy nights at the drive-in or parking on Booger Swamp Road—really knew. Or not so much a lack of what they knew, but a vocabulary that was up to the task of expressing it. There was, among those generally tough kids, a curious gentility in language, a refusal to face the full implications of what they were saying, a fear of the *word*. "Motherfucker," for example, generally came out "mullifucker." Or "roosterfish"—a favored term in good towel-snapping fun to call each other—instead of "cocksucker." It was as if they were afraid to use the term itself. It was too loaded.

As for another word of choice, "cornholing," we didn't know exactly what that meant, though, through context, we got some idea. For a year or so the senior jocks had a habit of coming up behind you in the hall and yelling "cornhole" as they grabbed your crotch from behind and tried to lift you off the ground. It hurt like hell, but soon even the freshmen got in the action, lurking behind hall lockers, then catching each other from behind, yelling "cornhole" and lifting up. Not until at least ten years later did I discover that "cornhole" did not mean exactly what we thought it did. I saw it in a novel somewhere, checked the Dictionary of American Slang or some such work, and found that it meant not "to grab one's crotch from behind" but instead "rough anal sex" or "anal rape." Obviously, our use of the word wasn't altogether off—an attack from behind was involved in both cases, usually male on male—but it was far from exact. In fact, never have I met anyone—veterans of Boy Scout troops, locker rooms, or basketball camps—who used the term "cornhole," if they used it at all, the way it had been used in Yadkin County. As usual, we didn't have it quite right.

But mainly, for a month or more in my freshman year, there was the matter of Dillinger's Dick—and in this, Yadkin County boys were not alone. I mean this in all seriousness: a friend of mine, a social historian at Brown University, has undertaken a study of the origins and meaning of the legend of near heroic Depression outlaw John Dillinger, and part of that legend concerns his outsized dong. *Did* he, in fact, have a whopper, as we all heard? Or was that widespread story just a projection of the wishes of legions of men in the 1930s who, thrown out of work and robbed of any semblance of masculinity, felt impotent in their own lives? Such are the matters my friend is investigating—in a book that, if on any other subject, would be subtitled something like "The Growth of a Legend."

To check out the Dillinger story, to see how far it went beyond Yadkin County, I recently did a little research of

my own. Of seven friends I asked—all male, having
grown up in places from California to New York to North
Carolina to Louisiana—only two had not encountered
the story of Dillinger's Dick at some point in their teens,
if not before. One who hadn't, curiously enough, was
from Dillinger's native Indiana, but this friend's refined
suburban Fort Wayne environs were a little more genteel
than the rougher places from which the rest of us sprang.
(I also asked three female friends; none claimed to have
heard of it.) There were variations on the tale: the exact
length varied, the means of its eventual extraction and
preservation, and its current location—for all had heard
that *it was still around,* pickled somewhere, in a jar. Some
had heard that the G-men had whacked it off after they
shot and killed Dillinger, others that it was removed at
the time of his autopsy. Some had been told, as I was by
some junior or senior, that it wound up in the Smithsonian (it is a fact that the Smithsonian has received hundreds of inquiries about it), some in FBI headquarters,
others at the Walter Reed. Whatever the case, this is serious business: how and why do legends grow?

And it was serious back in 1957 and 1958 in the Hornets' locker room as well, engendering awe, not to mention a virtual epidemic of penis envy. It remained, so to
speak, in the back of our minds, but there was also basketball to play. After my sophomore year and then two weeks
at Bones McKinney's summer basketball camp in eastern
North Carolina—where I first encountered a tall, skinny,
weird-looking but precocious kid named Pete Mara-
vich—and after growing three more inches, I approached
my junior year thinking things might be different. At six

feet even, I could now play forward, where I felt more comfortable. My leaping improved even more, particularly after we got what we called our jumping machine, a contraption that could be set at different heights for players to jump up and grab or tap the ball out. At first, I was able to tap it out a couple of inches over ten feet, which meant I could go a little over the rim, and by the end of the year at almost ten and a half feet.

We had a new coach too, one who promised to help improve our basketball fortunes. Billy Lyles was a short, stocky, curly-haired product of eastern North Carolina who had led Wake Forest to a Southern Conference title seven years earlier, one of the few times in those pre-ACC days when State's Wolfpack hadn't won. I had a picture of Lyles in my 1953 scrapbook, standing beside Dickie Hemric, over a caption that read, "Wake Forest hero ruffles the hair of Captain Billy Lyles." I didn't particularly like his Wake Forest pedigree, and he brought with him some strange notions—such as shooting free throws underhand—that he soon abandoned. He was also a firm believer in conditioning, running the dreaded lob-pass drill from one end of the court to the other till we dropped. But I thought he and his discipline, as well as his exposure to big-time basketball, would be good for us. He was a jaunty sort, confident and often jovial. "I'm William Otto Lyles," he would say. "Otto. Backward, Otto. Inside out, Toot." He also had a good-looking wife named Betty who picked him up after practice. When someone gave the signal she'd entered the gym, we'd sometimes burst out of the locker room, wearing only jocks, and do a lap around the gym in front of her. She barely noticed.

We had a quick senior guard named Doug Smith and a sweet-shooting sophomore named Steve Zachary starting along with the now 6'5" Crater, 6'2" Michael Adams, and me. We got off to a slow start, and in fact I remember very little about the first half of the season—other than some fans adding to their repertoire what they felt to be a timely cheer: "Two, four, six, eight / We don't want to integrate / Eight, six, four, two / We don't want no jiggaboos." North Carolina schools were finally on the verge of desegregation, five years after *Brown v. Board*. I remember that I didn't like the cheer, but I wasn't as indignant as I should have been, a reaction that suggests my benign neglect of those days. I didn't consider myself a racist—I disliked "Dixie" and the Confederate flag, and the word "nigger," not to mention "jiggaboo," had always been banned from my house—though, in fact, what else but racists were all white southerners in those days, even those of us who thought we weren't. In any case, at that point, I gave the matter no serious thought; that would have to wait a couple of years.

We came on very strong toward the end of the season, squeaked out a 63–62 win in the semifinals of the county tournament, and found ourselves facing seemingly invincible Jonesville in the finals. The Blue Jays were loaded as always, led by a 6'6" all-state player named Howard Pardue—a skinny long-range bomber with the best shooting touch anyone around here had ever seen. He carried himself like he knew how good he was; college scouts from all over the state and beyond were at the game, including one from Virginia Tech where Pardue would end up as a three-year starter.

But we were on a roll and feeling very confident for once, this time not even particularly intimidated by Jonesville. I had always played my best games against the Blue Jays, and I was ready again. With the gym rocking as we'd never heard it before, Steve Zachary and I had us even at the end of three quarters, and we thought we could hold on. We both were hitting from outside, and I was having my best rebounding game of the year. Until, in the fourth quarter, Pardue got hot, and there were no rebounds to get. We lost by four—heroically, it was reported to me that Plato Matthews had said in his radio broadcast—but nevertheless we lost.

The next week, in the western regional tournament, we reached the semi-finals. I recall only that I out-jumped a 6'6" guy to open the game, but then we went on to lose and the season was over. In any case, it was time—my father told me that spring—that I began to think about something other than basketball; in particular it was time to consider what I would do after high school. Aside from his strict attention to punctuality and good grammar, my father had pretty much let me go my own way. I'd made average grades—A's in English, social studies, and French but B's and C's in math and science—without his complaining too much, and he didn't push me at all in sports. He came to all home games, but if we were playing another team from Yadkin County he always sat on the visitors' side. "I'm superintendent of all the county schools, not just yours," he explained. "I can't show favoritism." That sounded reasonable enough to me, although not to the men of the Hornets' boosters club who thought he should support the school in the town where he lived, especially if his son was on the team.

But other things were on the horizon. It was assumed I would go to Carolina—though my grades weren't great, they would be good enough to get me admitted as an in-state student, and my place was secured when I made the highest SAT score in my class. What I would study at Chapel Hill was another matter. The only thing I was even remotely good at was writing, and there were precedents in my family. My father's first cousin Burke Davis had already made a name for himself as the author of a number of Civil War biographies and histories, and my mother's cousin Worth Tuttle Heddon had caused a stir in the 1940s and 50s with a couple of highly praised novels, one dealing with southern race relations, another based on intrigue in her own family. Besides, Thomas Wolfe was a Tar Heel from the hills and served as an inspiration for anyone in that area who even thought about writing. But to write, my father reminded me, I had to have something to *say*, and up to that point my mind was a blank. I had given up reading, my father pointed out, after that series of orange-bound biographies back in the fourth grade. I didn't read good fiction, or any fiction except the work assigned in my English class, and aside from my partisanship in presidential elections, I knew very little about what was really going on in the country. My parents couldn't even get me to look at the Huntley-Brinkley news each night.

But since I did know one thing, sports, and could write

about them, maybe I could be a sportswriter. In fact, I already was, to some degree: the previous fall I had written a column, "Hobson's Choice," for one of the county's two newspapers, making weekly college football picks and adding commentary. But what really turned me toward sportswriting was reading a *Winston-Salem Journal* writer named Bob Cole, and it wasn't so much what Cole said that impressed me but how he said it. It was the first time I had even paid any attention to *style* in writing, and if—as I was later told—you should first encounter Thomas Wolfe when you are eighteen and no older, encountering Bob Cole at sixteen was perfect for me. I have no idea what happened to the man after he left the *Journal.* I later heard he had been a graduate student in English at Wake Forest at the time he was writing sports, but whether he later joined the ranks of the professional *gelehrten* I don't know. He would now be about seventy or seventy-five, and for all I know he belongs to the ages. But he moved me mightily at the time.

I remember in particular one piece Cole wrote on Art Heyman, a two-time All-American at Duke. Heyman later bombed in the pros, and in later years he returned to Durham where he opened a hair-transplant emporium, "Art Heyman's Hair Connection." By the '90s I saw ads in the *Durham Herald* with a photo of a nearly bald Heyman side by side with a transplanted Heyman in full tonsorial splendor. I thought that a sad comedown for a man who in college had been simply magnificent, to that point the greatest player (Lennie Rosenbluth included) ever to play in the Atlantic Coast Conference. Cole had captured that magnificence in a long feature article entitled—what else—"King Arthur and His Court."

I didn't clip the piece and haven't seen it since, but I remember it very well. Basically what Cole did was tell the reader about Heyman's background—he was from Rockville Centre, New York, and was one of the few great Jewish players around (along with Rosenbluth)—and the figure he cut at Duke. But Cole did it in a way that made language stand up and perform, sing and dance and do tricks—in a manner not unlike that of the tour de force journalism Tom Wolfe was beginning to write, though at the time I'd never heard of *that* Tom Wolfe. After going on for a couple of thousand words, punning and playing the "King Arthur's Court" angle for all it was worth, Cole listed Heyman's achievements and concluded, in words I recall more than forty years later: "And that ain't hey, man. That's art." Today that might not qualify as the sublime, but, remember, I was sixteen, and Bob Cole, in his way, awakened me to the power of words—words not simply as a means to convey a message but things you can play with, have fun with. Others may have had loftier goals and more celebrated models: Flaubert, Joyce, Virginia Woolf, Faulkner. I had Bob Cole.

So sportswriting it would be, at least I thought at the time, and that solved another problem as well. I wanted to avoid anything—especially teaching and courtroom law—that involved a lot of public speaking, for as much as I loved playing basketball before an overflow crowd, I hated trying to speak. Since I was nine or ten I had had a stammer, a mild one as such things go, almost never bothering me in conversation but, by thirteen or four-teen, threatening to sabotage any classroom speech I gave. Not always. Sometimes I would sail right through. But at other times, despite preparation and attempts at positive thinking, I couldn't get the words out. I could never tell in advance whether I was headed for success or failure. Thus I learned early about the limits of self-determination, the vagaries of fate.

Others have written about the infuriating loss of con-trol involved in stammering—many, in fact, since the in-ability to express oneself in one medium, speaking, drives one even more to self-expression in another form, i.e., writing. John Updike, one of the afflicted, has given a lot of thought to "this anxious guilty blockage in the throat": "There is no doubt that I have lots of words inside me; but at moments, like rush-hour traffic at the mouth of a tunnel, they jam." Or, "My sensation, when I stutter, is that I am trying, with the machete of my face, to hack my way through a jungle of other minds' thrusting vines and tendrils." To the critic Alfred Kazin, rejected for service in World War II because of his stammer, "The word was my agony. The word that for others was so effortless and so neutral, so unburdened, so simple, so exact, I had first to meditate in advance, to see if I could make it, like a plumber fitting together odd lengths and shapes of pipes." As a student, when called on in class, Kazin "could never seem to get the easiest words out with the right dispatch, and would often miserably signal from [his] desk that [he] didn't know the answer rather than get up to stum-ble and fall and crash on every word."

For both Updike and Kazin, as for me, stammering

was an episodic thing, disappearing altogether for a time, then mysteriously reappearing. Both eventually came to feel reasonably comfortable speaking before large, impersonal groups (except, for Updike, New York ones), but both continued to be tripped up in other circumstances. For Updike, it was, among other things, "an electrician brusquely answering the phone, or a uniformed guard bristling at the entrance to a building, or a pert stranger at a cocktail party [who] does not know who I am, and I apparently doubt that my body and manner and voice will explain it." Updike finds the origins of his stammer in "some hasty wish to please," or some fear "of being misunderstood, of being mistaken for somebody else." He would even like to think, as Thomas Carlyle once wrote after meeting the stammering Henry James, Sr., "A stammering man is never a worthless one . . . It is an excess of delicacy, excess of sensibility to the presence of his fellow-creatures, that makes him stammer."

I'd like to think that too, though an "excess of sensibility" is a long way from describing my temperament in those early days. But I shared Updike's fear of being misunderstood, a fear that contributed mightily to the earliest episode of stammering I can recall. I was no more than eight or nine when an uncle—a large, hearty, jocular sort, as all Hobson uncles were—asked me who I was for, Duke or Carolina. He must have already known the answer, must have been kidding me, but I had to say it, had to get it out. The four syllables of Carolina were a lot harder than the one syllable of Duke, the hard "C" tougher than the "D," and after struggling for what seemed like a full minute, I finally blurted out "Duke." He reacted with great surprise, but I could explain no further. The humiliation of that moment is still with me.

For a time I almost envied those stammerers who skipped merrily along, Elmer Fudd style, saying g-g-go or p-p-put, always calling attention to their affliction, seeming never to be bothered by it. But I could go for weeks at the time without a slip, and almost never in conversation, which added even more pressure when I was called on in class or had to give a talk. The curious thing is that, from about the eighth grade on, I was the class cut-up, wisecracking, baiting the teacher. But *I* was in charge then, and the atmosphere was informal. When I had to stand up, solemnly, and read a passage, it was altogether different. Sometimes I could do it, sometimes I couldn't. And when I couldn't, there was none of that merrily-skipping-along stuttering. There was, rather, a great paralytic block, or at least it seemed that way to me—the inability to get *anything* out for several seconds. It was the kind of block, I realized when I later read Melville, that Billy Budd had when, falsely accused and unable to speak a word in his defense, he struck out at his accuser, Claggart, killing him with one blow.

The feeling I had at such moments of vocal paralysis—the tightness in the chest and the throat, the rush of adrenaline—was curiously the same feeling I had when I played basketball in front of a large crowd and was at my best. The adrenaline, even the tightness, focused me, made me jump higher, shoot better, react more quickly. And it didn't go away immediately when the game was over. In later years, in pickup games with players I didn't know, when I had played especially well and, after the game, other guys wanted to know who I was and where I had played before, I often couldn't get a word out. If I'd met these same people at a party, I could have talked with them for hours. But not just after basketball, when the adrenaline, the focus, hadn't worn off.

To this day I haven't figured out where my affliction came from. Was it some residual effect of polio (probably not) or the result of growing up with a father I wanted to please but from whom praise came infrequently (probably not: many other sons grow up in similar circumstance)? Or was it, as much current thinking holds, simply a physiological matter, a certain defect in vocal timing that, reinforced, turns into a habit? It is a fact that there is a much greater proportion of stammerers among writers than in the general population — among twentieth-century Americans, not only Updike and Kazin but also, at various points in their lives, Thomas Wolfe, John Dos Passos, and Delmore Schwartz, and, among the nineteenth- and twentieth-century British, Darwin, Arnold Bennett, Somerset Maugham, Elizabeth Bowen, Philip Larkin, and countless others.

In fact, among the English population as a whole, particularly the educated, there is a much greater propensity for stammering than among Americans — not only among writers and intellectuals but also kings (most famously, Queen Elizabeth's father, George VI, but, earlier, the beheaded Charles I: did *that* result from inadequate powers of vocal persuasion?) and commoners of various stations. As Kazin wrote, after a stay in wartime London, "Even the many upper-class stammerers I met among government officials and writers — people confidently directing the flow of English opinion—did not seem in the least impeded by their twitches, repetitions, mumblings, and nervous pauses. They just went on, even in public meetings, as if everyone in the audience knew what it was like to stammer. Might there be a bit of distinction to it?"

As for the correlation between writers and stammering, it's obvious there's no built-in gene that includes a propensity for both. A better guess is that with stammerers, even occasional ones, the necessity to cut your way through a verbal jungle, choosing any number of instruments—words—as you go, has the result of building a large vocabulary as well as a certain dexterity in using it. Not to mention the obvious fact that writing provides a means of self-expression for people cut off, to various degrees, from the usual means of public expression. It is a way to *perform* for those to whom other forms of performance—not only eloquence in public speaking but also drama and so forth—might seem to be closed. I don't think a dislike of public speaking *caused* me to want to write, but I do know that writing—and, even more (since the applause comes more spontaneously), basketball— brought me something I wanted very much: approval, which couldn't come, as it did for my father, through public speaking. Basketball, almost literally, spoke *for* me.

Like Updike's and Kazin's, my affliction stuck around, to some degree, for a long time, disappearing for months at a time, then presenting itself, like some cast-off relation you hoped you'd seen the last of, when you least wanted it to. After vowing I'd stay away from anything that involved public speaking, I ended up as—what else— a professor, and headed for American Literature, "American" being one of the toughest words to say when I was trapped. To this day, on those occasions when I accept a public speaking engagement (outside of my own class-room, where I found a certain comfort level), I never know for certain how it's going to go—sometimes smoothly but at other times, as Updike says, like hacking your way through a jungle.

But all that was to be in the future. Beginning my se-nior year I hardly gave speech a thought. I had finally grown—really grown—to 6'3", and both life and basket-ball were looking good. We had five of our top six players back from a team that had reached the county finals and the regional semis, and we had a coach who seemed to know what he was doing. All fall I worked on the jump-ing machine, getting so I could tap the ball out at almost eleven feet, and Coach Lyles said that was high enough to try to dunk. The only possible problem would be my grip: was my right hand big enough to palm the ball, to hold on to it as I launched myself toward the basket?

It was. Some time in early November 1960, about the same time Kennedy eked out his presidential victory over Nixon, I dunked for the first time—what would appear to be no big thing now, but it was a big deal then since no one in the history of our school had ever done such a thing. And dunking was like no sensation I had ever felt before. Aficionados of the art, in subsequent years, would often describe it in sexual terms, and pretty violent sexual terms at that. But they were talking about *slam* dunkers, the kind who, in jamming, could bend the rim and shatter the glass. To me at seventeen, dunking was more like flying, or rather it was like the ball was leading me up, pulling me up, and I was exerting very little effort myself.

I had an inside game now—could post up and whirl around my man for a layup or could pull up for a short jumper. Mainly, with my jumping—and having watched Elgin Baylor, the master of hanging in the air as long as he needed before releasing the ball—I realized I too could hang in the air longer than my defender and then put up my shot, twisting to the right, falling away, after the defender came down. "He shoots from his cods," complained Junior Steelman when Coach Lyles asked him why he couldn't stop me in practice, and I took that as a supreme compliment. Why couldn't I have been 6'3" all along, all four years, I thought. Whatever, I was now, and I still had the outside game as well—shooting, driving, passing, general court sense. Bones may have been right, after all.

The first game of my senior season was a rout, 56–31, over a team from the other side of Winston-Salem, and I hit for 26, more than I had ever scored before. The next was a 44–42 squeaker over a good Davie County team, at their gym, and I got 15, hitting three jumpers in the lane over their 6'6" center in the fourth quarter. We were looking like the team we had been forecast to be since the seventh grade, and I was having more fun than I'd ever had before. At home, in pregame warm-ups, the pep band played "Sweet Georgia Brown" and I dunked on demand. During games I would take my man inside and score, then move outside and hit from 18 or 20 feet, after which I would lope down the court, dangling my right hand (not *blowing* on it, as gunners in later years would do, just dangling it), holding it limp, like my hero Rosenbluth had done — dangling it as if it were some foreign object, not really of the same substance as the rest of me, delicate, sensitive, needing to rest until called on again. I dangled it, that is, until my coach, in that age of sexual stereotyping and gender insecurities, ordered me to cut it out.

During timeouts of games, both home and away, the cheerleaders — all those perky Peggys and Betsys and Sues, dressed in pleated skirts and bobby sox, bouncing up and down — would launch into their favorite cheer, which involved going through the names of the entire starting lineup, beginning with the least accomplished starter — "Jimmy, Jimmy, He's our man / If he can't do it, Michael can" — and so on, building toward the player they considered, at least for the moment, the worthiest, and thus deserving of the ultimate tribute. Last year I had been, at best, third or fourth from the end. But now, as I listened to Lyles's timeout instructions, I heard the sweet words filling the gym, "Freddy, Freddy, He's Our Man / If He Can't Do It / *Nobody* Can." Ah, never before had I been the last named, the chosen one.

So basketball was starting to have fringe benefits. Though I hadn't dated a lot my sophomore and junior years — I hated to use the telephone and asked girls out only when joking around in the hall — I finally had a real girlfriend, and from that seat of basketball aristocracy, Jonesville. She'd seen me light up her Blue Jays in the previous year's tournament final, had called me up and asked me out, and things had gone on from there. Like Jonesville hoopsters, Jonesville girls possessed a kind of mystique—not only prettier and classier but also more knowledgeable than the general variety in the county. A couple of Yadkinville football players, disregarding Roland's advice never to ride 'em bareback, had gotten pregnant a couple of prime specimens, so Jonesville represented danger as well as delight. No danger of that though, just yet, for the superintendent's boy, who wasn't to ride 'em, bareback or saddled, for another year or two.

So things were going well until the fourth game of the season, when our primary challenger for the county crown—other than lofty Jonesville—came to our gym. The Boonville Black Knights were led by my old Dixie Classic companion and rival Jay Martin, now a 6'5" star guard, and also starting for them was my first cousin Frank Hobson, a 6"4," 220-pound enforcer. Frankie was a farm boy, a football star, and generally a rough customer under the boards. He would go on in later years to become a prosperous tobacco farmer, and then, sensing America's choice of drugs was about to change—and after taking as his second wife a forward-thinking marketing genius—would replant his fields in grapes, largely cabernet and chardonnay, build himself a state-of-the-art winery, and become a celebrated vintner.

This later version of Frankie would have to wait until the 1990s and North Carolina's viticultural renaissance, at the center of which was to be none other than the Yadkin Valley, whose soil and climate were to be compared favorably, in certain wine-boosting publications I have seen, to that of both the Napa Valley and the Rhone. I'm not kidding. Frankie, whose wines would win a number of national awards, would come to be written up in newspapers across the state as a kind of Tar Heel Julio Gallo, his winery—named RagApple Lassie for his boyhood prize-winning Holstein calf—even making *Parade* magazine on one occasion. But it didn't go to his head. At summer Saturday concerts, which he came to put on in the midst of his vineyards, he threw in a dozen ears of corn if you bought a bottle of Boonville Blanc.

But in 1961 such visions of viticultural grandeur were far away for Frankie and the Black Knights. They came into our gym undefeated, as we were too, and it was the first really big game of the season. My Uncle Wade, a young lawyer whose sense of humor led him in strange directions, decided to turn the game into a personal contest between his two nephews. He called both of us the week before the game, passing on challenges allegedly sent by the other. On game night itself, as co-captain, I was to lead our team onto the court for warm-ups, and Uncle Wade was prepared for that too. As I made my way through the crowd at the end of the gym, my teammates behind me, he popped up from the side and knocked the ball out of my hand into the throng. After retrieving it, indignant at his interference, I dribbled the length of the court and dunked, but that didn't get rid of the humiliation. Neither did the game itself. The Black Knights jumped on us from the beginning, led all the way, and won 45–37 in a defensive struggle. I had my worst offensive output of the year, only seven points, and though a news story I recently unearthed says I was injured, I don't remember that. I just recall that I was outscored, outrebounded, and generally out-toughed by Frankie — who, along with Jay Martin, led the Knights in scoring.

Out-toughed: *that* was the problem, said Coach Lyles. He said I played "soft," lacked a mean streak, a killer instinct, wasn't hungry enough (or as John Edgar Wideman defines "soft" in *Hoop Roots*, "meaning [a player] didn't sufficiently assert or engage his physical endowments. Wasn't rough or tough enough . . . wasn't willing to work hard and diligently"). Up until that point Lyles and I had gotten along OK. He called me Hobsinger for some reason, but I rather liked that. (My teammates, aware of my jumping ability and given to racial stereotypes, changed it to "Hobnigger." Though I didn't like the moniker, I confess I appreciated the sentiment—since I'd tried to model my game on the players I sometimes saw at all-black Winston-Salem State.) Lyles had us over for hamburgers, showed us film of Wake Forest games in which he'd starred, and took us down to the Wake gym to practice. I even laughed at his "Toot" jokes. But the Boonville game changed everything. After that, in practice he singled me out for criticism, threw the ball—hard—at me when I wasn't expecting it, took me under the boards and, with his bulk, rooted me out for position—and once threw me out of practice.

At first it seemed to work. I had a streak of good games—22 against Sparta, 26 against West Yadkin, 34 against Courtney, 27 against Westfield, with double-figure rebounding in most of those games—and we won them all. I was averaging over 20 points a game, battling Jay Martin and two other players for the conference scoring title, and getting the kind of regional press coverage I had earlier dreamed about. Coaches from two or three small colleges in the state drove up to see me play. In the halls, between classes (though always watching my back, keeping a wary eye out for the random cornholer), I was having, at least by my lights, spectacular success lining up dates for the drive-in—quite literally, the only show in town—owned by my best friend's father. I was also still seeing my Jonesville girlfriend, and occasionally, from another town, a girl who read books in French and said she was going to Smith College—which I had never heard of. After the debacle against Boonville, all was now going better than I could have imagined. And, then, in late January, Jonesville—the team, not the girlfriend—came to town.

Although the Blue Jays had lost Howard Pardue, they were still the top team in the region, coming in undefeated. Two other stars, Paul Reynolds and Jerry Finney, had taken over where Pardue left off: both would later go on to solid college careers. We had won three of our last four—our last game a 50-point blowout—and we were ready. It was to be my best game of the year, particularly satisfying since I was guarded by Reynolds, a quick, spindly 6'4" leaper, the only other player in the county who could dunk. As the *Elkin Tribune* put it, I "was hitting from all angles, inside and out," and, to Lyles's satisfaction, was also getting position, controlling the boards, and playing defense—no longer playing "soft." We led 41–37 after three quarters, increased the lead at the beginning of the fourth and looked like we would take the Blue Jays for the first time in four years—until Reynolds and Finney got hot, John Mathis called on his coaching magic, and Jonesville pulled it out 61–58. I'd scored 30, but we'd lost the game I wanted to win more than any other.

It all went downhill from there. Our 6'5" center, Johnny Crater, had torn up his knee and was ineffective for the rest of the season. Steve Zachary, a 6'1" junior and a great offensive player, wasn't given the green light by Lyles often enough. Michael Adams and Jimmy Dobbins, all-conference football players who had also been promising basketball prospects earlier, hadn't panned out on the hardwood. The late-season frustration came to a head with a home game against East Bend, a strong team who had beaten us earlier at their place. This time we led most of the way, but they took the lead by one with fifteen or twenty seconds left. Lyles called time out, setting up a shot for me coming off a screen.

Dobbins, the point guard, was supposed to hit me on the right wing and I was to shoot or to drive, whichever looked best. I had been hitting all night, already had 24, and was in that unconscious zone in which a shooter knows he can't miss. I came off the screen, was wide open—but, instead of passing, Dobbins shot an air ball and the game was over. For me, it was to have been that winning shot at the buzzer that every player dreams of, the fantasy shot that always falls on a backyard court. I had never had a game-winning shot at the buzzer in a real game, and I was never to have a chance at one again. The next day in practice I got there early, picked up a ball, took it down to the exact place on the court I would have shot, took one dribble, and let fly. Swish!

The county tournament lay ahead, but as far as I was

concerned the season was over. We won easily in the first round, but were swamped by Jonesville 62–42 in the semifinals. Winning the third-place game the next night — in which the team as a whole played its best game of the year — didn't help. Neither did making all-county and all-region and ending the season averaging 20 a game. Neither did it help that the Boonville Black Knights, led as always by my old rival Jay and cousin Frankie, upset Jonesville in the tournament finals, won the western regionals, and headed for the state class A tournament in Durham, where Jay averaged more than 30 a game, led his team to within a point of the state championship, and got a basketball scholarship to Wake Forest for his spectacular performance.

And neither did it help much that Billy Lyles, the would-be savior of Hornets basketball, was fired — or quit, I'm not sure which — and as far as I know, left the game of basketball behind for good. He'd done us in, but we'd also done him in. If I took any satisfaction in that, it was balanced by the realization that in one important respect he had been right. For some reason, I hadn't been hungry, hadn't wanted it enough — though I'm not really sure it would have made any great difference if I had.

The Tuttles, all Duke, circa 1925. My grandfather, the football player, is front left; my
mother, age fifteen, center rear.

The Hobson clan, late 1930s. My father,
the tallest (second from right, back row),
his parents, brothers and sisters.

Miriam Tuttle Hobson, before my time, hiking Grandfather Mountain.

At first it was football.

Before the long-awaited growth spurt:
the author is in the center.

The backyard court and the woodpile.

1954: the author holding the ball.

In the spring
it was baseball.

Parents' day at summer camp for a home-
sick kid—who the next day won the Camp
Butler free throw championship.

1954: My parents, my older sisters, and me.

My parents' home, 1939–1994.

The Dixie Classic: "The greatest show on earth."

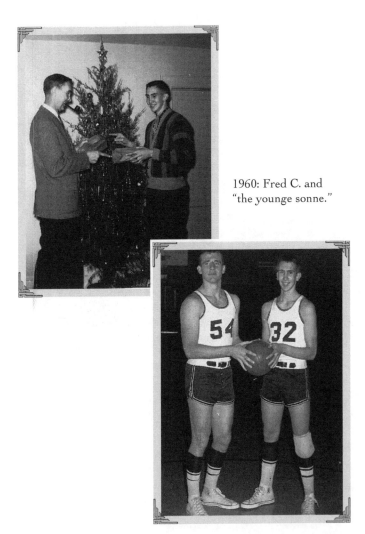

1960: Fred C. and
"the younge sonne."

High school co-captain (on right), in
need of upper body strength.

Perfect form,
but did it go in?

Scoring 30 against Blue Jays:
"Before the Celtics, before
UCLA, there was Jonesville."

126

The Tar Babies, 1961–1962, the "freshman team rated as the best ever at Chapel Hill" (*Sports Illustrated*). Billy Cunningham, rear, second from left; the Yadkin walk-on, rear, far right.

Sun Devil: without the game face.

Jane's matador defense: before
basketball overkill set in.

2005: the Boys of Winter.
The author is in the center.

6

Tar Baby

Among the nearly unbroken peaks of North Carolina basketball success—the conference and national championships, the 25- and 30-win seasons, the All-Americans, Olympians, and national players of the year—the early 1960s represents a relative valley, a brief period, between the national title of 1957 and three consecutive Final Fours of 1967–1969, of scaled-down expectations and comparatively meager achievements. The reason for the relative slump was a series of events in 1960 and 1961 that came as close to a scandal as Carolina basketball has ever experienced—among other things, a Tar Heel player suspected of ties to gamblers and game-fixers—as well as a general feeling among Chapel Hill administrators that the basketball atmosphere under Frank McGuire had gotten too big-time, or, to put it another way, had departed too radically from the Frank Porter Graham tradition of amateurism, of high thinking and plain living.

The results were that the best-in-the-nation Dixie Classic holiday tournament was suspended—it was to that super-charged event in Raleigh that many of the gamblers flocked—and that the basketball schedules for the two state-affiliated members of the ACC's Big Four, Carolina and N. C. State, were temporarily reduced by several games. Most disturbing to some Tar Heel faithful, in August 1961 McGuire resigned to become head coach of the NBA Philadelphia Warriors—some said, resigned under fire—and, in what was widely seen as a step toward deemphasis, the head coaching job was given to his little-known twenty-nine-year-old assistant, Dean Smith.

If this was deemphasis, you wouldn't have known it, given the hype that awaited the 1961–1962 freshman team—called by *Sports Illustrated* "the best ever at Chapel Hill." Other scribes said it was the best since the 1954–1955 freshman team of future national champions Pete Brennan, Joe Quigg, Tommy Kearns, and Bob Cunningham, but the point seemed clear: if this was a downturn for Carolina basketball, it was to be a brief one, to be reversed as soon as the '61–'62 freshman cagers moved up to the varsity. As *SI* predicted, "Look for [Carolina] to rebound into the national basketball limelight in the next season or so." The star recruits on the team, New Yorkers Billy Cunningham and Jay Neary, were McGuire's, but the Tar Babies also boasted the North Carolina high school player of the year before, Ray Respass, and two other indigenous high school stars, Bill Brown and Pud Hassell. If this had been the year before, the Tar Babies' coach would have been Dean Smith, but since Coach Smith had moved up to the head varsity job, we had Ken Rosemond, a native Carolinian and reserve guard on the '57 championship team.

Billy Cunningham, even then, was a phenomenon—

only a little over 6'4" (he later grew to 6'6" or 6'7") but with superb quickness, incredibly long arms, and the best leaping ability anyone in Chapel Hill had ever seen. When I first saw him, standing just off the court that first night of October tryouts, I wasn't overly impressed: with pasty white skin and what appeared to be soft, nearly hairless legs, he wasn't physically imposing, was, in fact, rather strange looking. But the amused half-smile he wore, a look that suggested he was toying with the rest of us, told us how good he knew he was, and when he took the court I realized he was right.

It was no wonder Cunningham was called the finest Carolina recruit since Lennie Rosenbluth—and that included, in between, All-Americans Lee Shaffer, Doug Moe, and York Larese—or that Rosemond said in an early newspaper interview that he "could become the greatest we've ever had here." Cunningham played what many at the time called "black basketball"—which meant he possessed astounding hang-in-the-air moves, the kind I had employed my last high-school year, only his were a hundred times better. At basketball-rich Erasmus Hall High in Brooklyn he had set the school scoring record of 61 points in a game, and not only had he enrolled early at Carolina the spring before but he had also decided to remain after McGuire left and Smith took over. Rosemond was right: Cunningham would become the finest Carolina player to that point (only Rosenbluth would challenge him), and later, after his pro career, would be named one of the fifty greatest NBA players ever.

The other recruits weren't as spectacular as Cunningham, although Respass—an eastern North Carolinian

who, Coach Rosemond said, had "the potential to become the best native North Carolina boy in Big Four history"—sometimes came close. As for the walk-ons, Bill
Taylor, a 5'11" guard with maturity, court sense, and a
sweet jump shot, was better than the rest of us. Most of
the other walk-ons were North Carolina high school
stars, most more publicized than I was and, as it turned
out, probably better all-around players. Coach Rosemond was very high on the native walk-ons. As he said
after a couple of weeks of practice, he could let Cunningham and Neary go, also let the home-state scholarship players go, take just the native Carolina walk-ons,
and still beat any other freshman team in the country.
That proved to be far from true, but it was nice to hear.
Freshman teams were all about hope anyway, and potential and dreams—the future. That's the reason we were
followed so closely that season, a year the varsity would
lose as many games as it won. At times we got almost as
much press coverage, and had as many fans turn out for
our games, as they did.

I have already described my own overachieving week
of tryouts. After that, I was briefly the seventh man, the
top front-court reserve, but soon I returned to mediocrity. Dunks looked good in warm-ups, but they were almost impossible to execute, at least for me, in practice or
in games. Fifteen- and twenty-foot jump shots which I'd
hit, largely unguarded, in tryouts, were a lot tougher with
Cunningham's or Respass's hand in my face. Shot-blocking
looked good, but other players soon learned I'd go for the
pump fakes, and they'd leave me hanging in the air while
they slithered around me for layups. As for rebounding, I

soon realized that boxing out—getting good position—
was far more important than jumping, and I lacked both
the strength and the savvy to keep Cunningham and
Respass, or even Pud Hassell and Bill Brown, off the
boards. There were brief moments of glory in those late
October and November practices—once, blocking a
Cunningham layup from behind, off the board, as he
loped downcourt for an easy layup—but those moments
were far outnumbered by defensive lapses, poor ball-
handling, failures to box out and set picks, and a general
lack of *toughness* seemingly bred in the big-city boys.
Those Durham accusations of six years earlier came back
to me: *"Country boy."* I was far from ready for prime time.

I noticed as practice continued that fall that Coach
Smith, though elevated to the varsity, still stopped by a
lot to watch the freshmen, probably drooling over what
he'd have next year when Cunningham became eligible.
My earliest impressions of the man who would go on to
become the winningest college coach of all time were
something less than overwhelming, and I think almost all
of us felt that way. He was an extremely kind and decent
man, a disciplinarian but an eminently fair one, and those
who later said that he treated his lowliest reserves with as
much respect as he did his stars were absolutely correct.
But, after the charismatic Frank McGuire, Coach Smith
seemed to lack star power. With his small stature, his
Kansas twang, and a mathematician's commitment to pre-
cision, he seemed in these early days, before he achieved
the distinguished bearing of his later years, a figure only
two or three steps up from what twenty years later might
have been called a nerd—a sort of Joe Paterno of the

hardwood. (As a large scrawled message on the overpass between Duke's east and west campuses put it, "Dean Smith wears ugly ties.") In any case, he seemed a figure not *formidable* enough to restore Carolina's basketball fortunes. And this is the impression of Smith that would remain, to some extent, for five or six years to come — through several mediocre seasons, through an especially rough period when he was hanged in effigy by some Carolina fans. There seemed little to suggest the greatness that lay in store.

But what they all missed, and what I missed too in the beginning, was the steel in the man, the toughness, and the extent to which a first-rate intellect could be applied to basketball strategy. It could be seen in the very beginning, in fact, for those who looked hard enough. There was no way his varsity team that first year — which featured slick guard Larry Brown and a rugged Pennsylvanian named Jim Hudock, but didn't have a lot more — should have broken even. Especially, there was no way, the following year, that Coach Smith should have taken his undermanned team into Lexington and beaten Adolph Rupp's Kentucky Wildcats. Or beaten Duke at all during those first four or five years. The way he did it was through strategy — particularly, the first year or two, with his shuffle offense, which overcame his team's lack of size by having *all* his undersized players pass and cut into the lane, utilizing their speed and quickness; and then, a few years later, turning to a four-corners offense that stressed ball possession and getting the best shot possible.

And there was no way you could fully gauge, in that

first year or two, just how much Coach Smith's players would want to win for him, would (with Smith the cliché was true) sacrifice themselves for the team. Many years later, when ESPN would honor Dean Smith as the greatest coach in any sport, at any level, of the last quarter of the twentieth century, many were the commentators who issued a virtual hagiography of the man, focusing not so much on his championships and his All-Americans but on his *character*, all to such an extent that the uninformed listener, in an age of hype, would probably have turned away and said "Yeah, sure." Except with Coach Smith, it was true. If any American coach stood for those old-fashioned values of teamwork and discipline and self-sacrifice, it was Smith. To this day I believe that to Coach Smith there *were* certain things more important than winning (I cringed in later years when I considered some of the weak but character-building lineups he put on the floor at crucial moments of crucial games—say, in the waning minutes of the 1993 national title game with Michigan), but he was also, beneath the kindness and decency, as competitive as any coach has ever been.

But all the records, the idolatry, were to lie in the future. All of us saw the decency but few of us, if we are honest, saw the greatness that was to come. Neither did we see, since he was quiet about it, the social commitment that Coach Smith later would be hailed for. During the early sixties, while he was helping to integrate Chapel Hill—on one occasion, single-handedly, breaking the color barrier in a local restaurant by taking a black player to dinner—most of his players, including me, lacked his high-mindedness. Getting by in the classroom, getting through practice every day, maybe getting lucky on Saturday nights—that's all we had on our minds.

What I remember mostly about those autumn afternoon practices in Chapel Hill isn't the toughness of the workouts (in fact, we ran less than we had in high school) or the basketball wisdom of Ken Rosemond but rather what might be called the sociology of the gym—and this pertained more to the varsity than to the freshman team. I was a small-town boy from an all-WASP county, after all, and when we came into practice the upperclassmen— a mixture of New York Irish Catholic (Bryan McSweeny, Donnie Walsh, Jim Donahue, Peppy Callahan) and Jewish (Larry Brown and Artie Katz) players, with an Italian American (Billy Galanti) and a German American (Dieter Krause) and an Eastern European (Jim Hudock) thrown in—were still on the floor. These were still McGuire's boys, and they were among the last of the '50s coalition of Catholics and Jews that he'd brought down on his underground railroad—to be succeeded in a very few years by Smith's own mixture of white Pennsylvanians and Ohioans and Hoosiers (both Protestant and Catholic), as well as African Americans both from New York and the South.

In 1961–1962, those latter days of the New York Catholic-Jewish diaspora, I remember, among the practice sounds in Woollen Gym, over the cacophony of coaches' whistles and squeaking Converses and the constant cries of "Hands" (meaning, hands up and active on defense) and "Ball" and "Go," hearing the New York accents, so strange to my Tar Heel ears—Larry Brown, for example, yelling downcourt to Dieter Krause, pronouncing it "Dee'-ta," so much more precise than the flat, lazy, rhythmless "Dee'-der" that emerged from my own southern lips. Most of the New Yorkers on the '57 team had come from Brooklyn and Queens and the Bronx; most of them now came not from the City but rather from Long Island—places like Long Beach and East Meadow, Glen Cove and Valley Stream. I'd never seen Long Island, of course, but to me, innocent of the general American practice of naming a new suburb or subdivision for the part of nature destroyed or displaced in its creation (Oak Grove or Brookwood, Orchard Park or Hidden Valley), such places sounded absolutely idyllic.

The varsity, as I recall, usually practiced just before we did, and as we waited to take the court, I heard more of the New York talk, from Cunningham and Jay Neary, as well as the general brand of jocular, all-in-it-together banter that you hear in any locker room. Here, about half the time, I was "Freddy"—a designation I had tried to get away from back in high school, seeing it as a name right out of Oscar Wilde, a fat, pimple-faced English schoolboy sort of name—but here, among the Tar Babies, the Billys and Timmys and Puds, I found I rather liked it. I even came to like the corny pep talks Coach Rosemond gave us—including one, before we faced an especially weak opponent in a preseason exhibition game, that he said he had heard in Frank McGuire's locker room in the '57 season. It went something like this: "You may not think this team you're playing tonight is any good, that it'll be a cakewalk. But I was passing through their locker room on the way over here. I saw their uniforms on the bench, and I saw they had jocks. If they have jocks, that means they have balls. If they have balls, that means they are men. And if they are men, they can beat you. So (PAUSE), let's go get 'em!"

When the season itself began, Coach Rosemond needed no pep talks. We were ready to go—in our first game, before a sellout crowd in Woollen Gym, beating the Virginia Cavayearlings,* 91–74, with Cunningham and Neary each getting 24 points. There, in the game program, I was, between No. 22, Jay Neary, Cambria Heights, N.Y., and No. 32, Billy Cunningham, Brooklyn, N.Y.: "30 Fred Hobson 6–3 180 Yadkinville N.C." My best moments that night, though, were not in the game itself but in pregame warm-ups, taking the court under the bright lights on the same floor where Rosenbluth had played, hearing the cheers as we came onto the floor (largely for Cunningham, but the rest of us pretended otherwise), doing the one thing I could do well—dunking. It has occurred to me since that my role in the Tar Baby show would have been reduced even further if the no-dunking rule during warm-ups, which was enacted a few years later, had been around in 1961–1962: that was the only way I had to shine. I got off a few good ones that

* "Cavayearlings" is really what they were called—just as the South Carolina [Gamecock] freshmen were called the Biddies, the Davidson [Wildcat] freshmen the Wildkittens, and the Duke freshmen the Blue Imps. As for Tar Babies, that was a natural for fledgling Tar Heels. In contemporary folklore circles, to students of Uncle Remus and Brer Rabbit, the term might seem to be tinged with racism, but as far as I know, Carolina fans—black as well as white—have never read it that way. With the end of freshman teams in the early 1970s, the term "Tar Baby" largely disappeared from Tar Heel vocabularies.

night, then took my seat, two or three down from Coach Rosemond, and there, except for a halftime break, I sat almost the entire game. So, except for sixth-man Bill Taylor, did all the other Carolina walk-ons—those stalwarts who Rosemond had said could beat any other freshman team in the country. Only with the game well in hand, with four minutes left, did we get in. I didn't score, and as I recall I got only a rebound or two. That was it.

But that wasn't bad, I decided, already settling into my Tar Baby complacency, happy just to be part of such a fine bunch whether I was playing much or not. For the Virginia game I had resorted to my old high school trick—getting a date for the game, putting her in the stands while she watched me play (or, in this case, not play), hoping she was impressed by two-handed warmup dunks. It was a new meaning of foreplay, but the one I knew best at the time. For the Cavayearling game my date was Charleen, a tall dark-haired girl who, I remember thinking at the time, wouldn't have gone out with such a socially inept small-town boy if he hadn't been a Tar Baby.

But basketball was opening doors, and not just with Charleen. I had barely learned how to drink (though I knew now what Larry Brown had meant by "get your stomach lined") and I had better moves on the court than with Chi O, Tri Delt, and KD pledges at fraternity parties—to which, since I looked about sixteen, I suspect I never would have been invited in the first place if I hadn't been a basketball player. But I did get invited, and found that playing, or sitting, for the Tar Babies also brought other perks. We got seats behind the bench for all varsity games (all the better to be seen on television during time-outs), two free tickets to do with what we wanted, the huge steak and baked potato we always had for the pre-game meal, and five dollars in meal money for afterwards. And there was recognition, even for bench-sitters: when I walked across campus the week after the Virginia game, I heard "good game" from four or five people I didn't know—though, for me, it hadn't been that at all.

We played only two other games in December, beating a poor Elon team 90–48, then traveling to the outskirts of Charlotte to beat a very good Davidson team, full of all-stars recruited by the young and ambitious Lefty Driesell, 67–63. I loved the road trips, cruising across the state of North Carolina, wearing my navy blazer with "University of North Carolina" on the breast pocket, stopping in good restaurants and getting noticed. On especially cold nights I wore the Harris Tweed topcoat my father had bought me that fall, sticking to his credo that every man should have one. I now see how ridiculous I must have looked, an eighteen-year-old kid, looking two years younger, a small crew-cut head sticking out of a bulky overcoat. But my father was right that Harris Tweed topcoats would last: forty years later I'm still wearing the same one.

After the Davidson game we had a long break from classes, which meant practice twice a day, while all other students went home early for the holidays. After our own abbreviated Christmas break we were supposed to report back in late December, a week or so before classes resumed, for more two-a-days, preparing for a rigorous January. For some reason I can't recall I came back two days late—and paid the price by being demoted from seventh or eighth to ninth man. Why had I done that, I later wondered, other than not wanting to face a cold, lonely dorm room and two hard practices a day? *Why*— after earlier wanting more than anything to make the team? Had Coach Lyles been right after all: was I not hungry enough?

It was obvious that the Tar Babies wouldn't suffer at all from my brief desertion. In early January we went to Wilmington and beat a loaded Wilmington College team in overtime, and then won 73–70 over N.C. State at Raleigh. We were now 5 and 0 and, led by Cunningham, were getting more and more attention all the time. Since my demotion, I wasn't playing much, but neither were the other walk-ons except for Bill Taylor. None of us was scoring much, and we weren't playing at all in most of the close games. Still, it was great to be along for the ride. At State's Reynolds Coliseum, the site of my earlier Dixie Classic autograph-seeking, I was actually approached by a couple of kids after the game wanting my autograph. Obviously they thought I was someone else, someone good, but I obliged anyway, and even wrote, as Rosen- bluth had for me six years earlier, "Best wishes"—and then thought of the disappointment of those two Raleigh kids when they would later look at their programs and find a name all but unrecognizable.

The winning streak continued in the following weeks, although the next win was one that may have been my bitterest disappointment of the year. On the morning of the day in mid-January that we were to travel to Winston-Salem to play the Wake Forest Baby Deacs—

the game, in this case, to precede the varsity game — the
Carolina Piedmont was hit by its biggest snowfall of the
year. We couldn't take the bus eighty miles west on un-
scraped roads, and as it turned out Coach Rosemond
took only six players and the team manager in a couple of
cars with chains on them. He had called around that
morning saying to be at Woollen Gym at noon, but I hadn't
got the message, and I arrived at the gym about a half
hour after the cars had left. That wouldn't have mattered
greatly ordinarily — but this game was in Winston,
twenty-five miles from my home, and my parents and a
lot of hometown friends had tickets. I had worked myself
back up to seventh man and would get to play against my
old rival Jay Martin, who was sixth man for the Deacs.
But there was no way to get to Winston-Salem, and I
missed the game. That we won in a blowout, 79–58, made
it all the worse; that meant I would have got a lot of playing time.

Two nights later, a Friday, came the biggest game of
the year, this one at home against Duke. The Blue Devils,
coached by Vic Bubas and starring All-Americans Art
Heyman and Jeff Mullins, were a powerhouse in those
days, and so were their freshman teams of the late '50s
and early and mid '60s. The Carolina-Duke basketball rivalry would later come to be celebrated — as Will Blythe
has written in *Sports Illustrated* — as "the greatest rivalry in
college athletics, perhaps in all of sports." Although it
hadn't quite reached that Homeric stage in the 1960s, it
was getting there, and the rivalry extended to the freshman teams as well.

The Blue Imps came into Woollen Gym with a 22-game

winning streak over the past two years, and the place filled up long before the game was to start. Featuring Hack Tison, a slender but talented seven-footer from Illinois, the Imps were bigger at every position than the Tar Babies, but that seemed to matter little this particular night. The 6'4" Cunningham, already called the Kangaroo Kid, outjumped Tison to begin the game, and after Billy picked up his fourth foul just before the half, Pud Hassell, at 6'3," shut Tison down the rest of the game. We led at the half 32–31, then Duke took a 36–32 lead, then we battled back with Cunningham on the bench. When he returned to the game, we scored twelve straight points to put it away. It was a glorious victory, and the fans rushed the court. Except for Bill Taylor, the walk-ons hadn't played a minute — I hadn't taken the court except for pregame and halftime warmups — but it didn't seem to matter at all.

The Duke win was our eighth in a row, and the next two, easy wins over South Carolina and N.C. State, both in Chapel Hill, made the ninth and tenth. "Freshman basketball is a major league sport at UNC," one North Carolina paper wrote, and national sports pages, noting the unbeaten streak, said the same thing. But those articles in mid and late January contained one other salient fact: Cunningham, because he had enrolled the spring before, would be held out the spring semester, beginning in early February, so he would later be eligible for three full years of varsity ball. I'm not sure we fully realized what that meant: I think Coach Rosemond had convinced us — what else was he to do? — that we could continue to win big without Kangaroo. Selfishly I might even have halfway welcomed his leaving the team, because it would mean more playing time for me and a couple of other walk-ons.

It *would* have meant more playing time, that is, if I hadn't blown it again. I did the same thing I had done at Christmas, stayed home an extra day during late-January semester break, rather than returning on time for two-a-day workouts before classes began. Having again risen to sixth or seventh man, I was again put back to nine or ten—and was lucky not to be thrown off the team completely. Again there was no good reason—looking back, even now, I don't know why I did it. Laziness. Complacency. Immaturity. The realization that I wouldn't ever be good enough to start, no matter how hard I worked—although, now that Cunningham was gone, I could have (in my father's favorite word, and one of Coach Smith's) *contributed*. Apparently having made the team was enough, being recognized on campus, signing an autograph or two, getting the meal money.

But there it was—and such carelessness, in fact, characterized almost everything about my first semester at Chapel Hill. My grades came in when I was home during the break, and they were dismal: three Cs (English, French, Modern Civilization) and Ds in math and botany. The botany grade, D-, had been a gift: I had never been able to see anything through the microscope. (Cunningham, by contrast—proving that a tree did grow in Brooklyn—got a C in botany.) I had all sorts of excuses for my parents—road trips, daily practice, being too tired to study at night. But in fact I had no idea *how* to study, no intellectual curiosity at all, absolutely no interest in the life of the mind.

Neither did I have any interest in what was going on around me in Chapel Hill. The University of North Carolina was widely regarded as the center of southern liberalism and social activism, and any number of prominent speakers had come to campus that fall. Aside from President Kennedy in October, I had heard none of them. The civil rights movement, which had begun its '60s phase nearly two years before only fifty miles up the road in Greensboro, had quickly spread to Chapel Hill, and by 1961–1962 the movement was well established. Almost daily, demonstrators picketed the segregated Varsity and Carolina theaters—and I paid virtually no attention.

My excuse, other than basketball, would have been that I had had a rough semester, moving from Cobb Dorm and my strange Yankee roommate a week or two after the murder-suicide across the hall, and then enduring two other bizarre roommates. The first, who envisioned himself a southern Holden Caulfield—he was always quoting *Catcher in the Rye*—dropped out after a month or so and returned to south Florida, only to turn up on my TV screen at Thanksgiving, then throughout the winter, in a Vitalis ad—as the boy who used the greasy kid stuff—with golfer Doug Sanders. The other roommate played bridge until three in the morning; I remember him only for that and for his firm conviction that NASCAR should be an Olympic sport. All these things I had to deal with, but the fact remained: if I didn't get my grades up spring semester, I would flunk out of Carolina.

So I returned from semester break duly admonished by my father—who did not seem overly concerned by my basketball transgressions, or even particularly by my bad grades, but more about my failure to take advantage of the social and cultural riches of Frank Porter Graham's Chapel Hill. Two days after I got back, three days after everyone else had, the Tar Babies headed for Duke Indoor Stadium for a Saturday night rematch of the earlier Chapel Hill barn-burner. It was a game loaded with meaning for me, reason enough, you might think, for me to have come back in time for practice. Not only was this to be a rematch of the two freshman teams some saw— unrealistically, as it turned out—as the best in the country, but my closest cousin Robert Tuttle, both friend and rival for as long as I could remember, was a junior at Duke and had tickets for the game.

Two years older than I was, Robert had been the closest thing to a big brother I had, living fifty or sixty miles away but spending weeks with me in the summer while his parents, my Uncle Bob and Aunt Lillian, gallivanted off to Yugoslavia, and later Iran, to visit Aunt Lillian's brother, the U.S. ambassador. A city boy, Robert—now "Bob" at Duke—was far cooler than I could hope to be in any foreseeable future. Straight from central casting, there he was, as the Tar Babies entered the gym, walking up to me, in his Duke blue v-neck cashmere sweater with an ATO pin on his chest and a gorgeous blonde on his arm. Assuming the air of authority he'd cultivated since entering college, two years before me, he put his arm around my shoulder, pulled me close, and whispered that the Blue Imps would get revenge.

It wasn't even close, in fact: the Tar Babies, who were among the country's two or three best freshman teams with Cunningham, seemed distinctly average without him. The Blue Imps, with proto-Cameron Crazies (they wouldn't actually get that name for another twenty years) cheering them on, jumped off to a big lead, were in front 38–29 at halftime, and ending up routing us 81–60. Without the Kangaroo Kid, we were overwhelmed on the front line; our starters were 6'4", 6'3", and 6'3", theirs 7'0", 6'7", and 6'5", and it showed in the rebounding margin, 52–30. Desperate, Coach Rosemond tried everything, including playing me more than I'd played in several games. Finding the Duke floor especially springy, I got several rebounds but did nothing else. Our ten-game winning streak came to an end—and with it Pud Hassell's 86-game streak, built over three high-school state championship years and the first half of the freshman season.

I got more playing time the rest of the season, a result partly of finally buckling down in practice but mainly of Rosemond's desperation. After losing a second game, to Davidson, a team we'd beaten on their home court two months earlier, Wake Forest came to town for a rematch. Again we won handily, and again I missed a game I really wanted to play—both because it would be another chance to play against Jay Martin and because my parents came down for the game. The reason this time was not the weather but what university sports administrators would later call "the academic side": the game was scheduled for noon on Saturday, to precede the varsity game, and the pregame meal, always four hours in advance, was scheduled for 8 a.m., the very time I had a French class. Keeping my fall grades in mind, I felt I couldn't cut. I went to class, assuming the pregame meal didn't really matter that much, but when I showed up at the gym about 9:30 I found I was suspended for the game. I couldn't even dress, couldn't sit on the bench, couldn't put on my show in warm-ups. I protested that this was *French* class, not oversleeping, but to no avail. Coach Rosemond said I had to get my priorities straight.

The next game, a third win of the season over N.C. State, put us at 12–2, but, again in the doghouse, I didn't get a lot of playing time. I got much more the following game, a close loss to Wilmington College — our third to a team we had beaten the first half of the season. I got several rebounds and hit a twenty-foot jumper to give us a brief lead midway through the second half, but I remember the game primarily for two things. First, Wilmington had a sharpshooting forward named Walter Jones, who some thirty years later would become a North Carolina congressmen, one notable largely for proposing "freedom fries" on the House cafeteria menu during the Iraq War, and also for conducting a vendetta against Chapel Hill professors who, he charged, indoctrinated their students with liberal propaganda. Second, if I'm not mistaken, it was the first basketball game my friend Curry Kirkpatrick — then a freshman from upstate New York, later *Sports Illustrated*'s leading basketball writer and a master of the New Journalism — covered for the *Daily Tar Heel*. Curry was no threat to Tom Wolfe yet. The last words of his first basketball article were pretty basic: "Fred Hobson, in a relief role, hit his only field goal attempt for the Tar Babies' other basket."

After that, only one game remained, a big one, against Duke, for the ACC freshman championship. We both were 6–1 in conference play, had split our previous two games, and were playing the grudge match in an 8 p.m. feature game before a full house in Woollen Gym. Again, without Cunningham, we were outmanned, but we made it close all the way. It came down to the last minute, the Blue Imps leading 65–64, and we had the ball. I was on the bench—the five starters having gone almost all the way—and I wanted badly to be in the game and take the shot. I was certain I could hit from outside. But, of course, I hadn't earned it. Pud Hassell shot from twenty feet and missed, Duke got the rebound, hit a couple of free throws, and it was over, 67–64. After winning ten in a row and being touted as the best around, we had lost four of our final six and ended the season in ignominy. The heart, in fact, had gone out of our season long before Duke beat us that final game, had departed back in early February when Cunningham left the team.

It was the beginning of March anyway, and spring was coming to Chapel Hill, and most of us were tired of practice. But, first, there was a kind of debriefing for all of us, an individual meeting with Coach Rosemond in which we discussed our prospects—or lack of them—for the future. I also met with Coach Smith to confirm what was obvious to anyone who had observed my less than stellar freshman year: that I had very little chance to make the varsity the following year. I remember well what he said, and in fact find his comments now in a yellowed letter that I wrote home to my parents that spring: "Coach Smith said when he and Coach Rosemond first saw me in

frosh practice, they thought I was a real discovery."
What wasn't said—but what Coach Smith certainly implied—is that after that I had been a great disappointment. "I found out I should have hustled more," I wrote
my parents, but that and "needing better work habits"
hadn't been the only problems. In a statement that puzzled me at the time, and took me two or three decades to
figure out completely, Coach Smith said I had "more athleticism than skills," which he didn't mean as a compliment. He confirmed what I'd thought—my chances weren't
good—but he surprised me by adding that I should work
on my game over the summer and then at least try out in
the fall. It was late March when we talked, the drudgery
of practice nearly a month in the past, and trying out
again, futile as it might be, sounded good.

Two or three weeks later we had our annual basketball
banquet, sharing the evening with the varsity, which in
Coach Smith's first season—under the reduced schedule
restrictions—had gone only 8 and 8. The banquet was a
big deal, because the speaker was to be Frank McGuire,
who had just completed his first season coaching Wilt
Chamberlain and the Philadelphia Warriors. It was my
first full appreciation of what Grant Wahl, writing much
later in *Sports Illustrated*, was to call "the Carolina family
. . . the most storied clan in college basketball." In fact,
the family was then in its infancy, and was hardly the
most storied clan at that point. But at least two or three
players from the '57 national championship team were on
hand—Joe Quigg and Danny Lotz, I know, and I think
someone else—but not Rosenbluth. As for the coaches, it
was a sort of apostolic succession, a laying on of hands:

McGuire, the coach of the '57 champions, coming back to give his blessing to Dean Smith, the assistant he had hired just after that '57 championship game and the man (himself with deep historical roots, having played at Kansas for Phog Allen, who had played under James Naismith, the founder of basketball) who would go on to surpass McGuire in Tar Heel lore and become the winningest college coach in history.

I was, of course, little better than a stepchild, the lowest of the low, in that family—I and Bill Vick and George McLean and Stu Ellington and the other Carolina schoolboys who had been lucky enough to make the team as walk-ons. But there I was, soaking it up, being recognized and tokenly applauded, getting my letter jacket, along with the other freshmen. And there was McGuire—who had written me the letter seven years before, saying if I worked hard and so forth, I would be good enough to play for Carolina. Well, not quite, at least not much, but still I was sitting there. I have forgotten completely what McGuire said in his talk—probably some 1960s version of that later coachspeak about giving 110 percent and leaving it all on the floor—but I do know that after the speech I was tempted to go up to him and tell him about the letter I had written him in 1955 and the nice note he had written back. I thought about it, but of course I didn't do it. Not with Coach Smith and Joe Quigg and Cunningham and Larry Brown standing around him. Not a chance. That would not have been cool at all. And besides, all of that had been a long time ago.

Over the summer of 1962 I did practice every day, after working from seven to five for the Yadkin County school maintenance crew, moving desks, painting classrooms, and digging ditches. I worked out in the Yadkinville gym for an hour or two, alone—nobody else was interested in playing basketball in the summer—but the things I worked on, shooting and dunking, were the things I already did well. It's hard to set picks and box out and move your feet on defense when you're all by yourself. Which made it, in one sense, an indoor version of the backyard fantasy basketball I had played as a kid—only now with the summer heat in the unair-conditioned gym, the late afternoon sunlight coming through the high windows and highlighting stirred-up particles of dust. But I loved the solitude, running the court, pulling up and firing from twenty feet. I ran a lot and, with the maintenance crew work, I got stronger.

In September I was ready to return to Chapel Hill. My grades had been much better the previous spring, so I was in no danger now of flunking out and could look forward to October tryouts, though with no great expectations. This October, like the one before, basketball tryouts seemed a pale reflection of—or, more accurately, a welcome distraction from—a greater drama being played out beyond Woollen Gym. The year before the drama had been local: the murder-suicide in Cobb Dorm, the continuing fear and mystery surrounding it, and the visit, days afterward, of President Kennedy. This year the drama, the Cuban missile crisis, was more cosmic. As practice got under way in mid-October, we had one eye on the hardwood and the other on Washington and Kennedy's eyeball-to-eyeball confrontation with Khrushchev.

This time the term "tryouts" wasn't exactly correct. Although there had been eighty or ninety players out for the freshman team the previous year and there were just eighteen or nineteen for the varsity now, the numbers were deceiving. These players were a whole lot better. In fact, the Carolina team was pretty well set for the year, with ten lettermen returning from last year's varsity, along with one redshirt (then called, for some reason, a "bohunk"), and the four sophomores who had started for last year's freshman team. (The fifth, Jay Neary, had gone back to New York.) That made fifteen players, all of them on scholarship, and fifteen was the number of players Coach Smith could carry on the team. So, unless someone got hurt, neither I nor the other two sophomore walk-ons seemed to have a chance. We understood that completely: Coach Smith had called Bill Vick and me into his office the first day and told us the odds were against us, but that we should go all out, far more than we both had last year, and we'd see what happened.

In a sense, that made it more fun—absolutely nothing to lose, and since we would probably be let go within a couple of weeks there was not that dread of the endless drudgery of practice. Coach Smith, true to his reputation, treated all the players, scholarship and walk-on, the same, putting us through the same drills, giving us all equal playing time. There were stars—team captain Larry Brown, back as a senior, and Cunningham, already heading for All-American as a sophomore—but, other than always playing Larry and Cunningham in a unit with the three other likely starters, Coach gave them no special treatment.

I can't recall many details about those first days of practice, but I find a few in a letter I wrote my parents during the middle of the first week: "I looked good the first night, fair last night, and really good this afternoon. This afternoon I scored eight points, got four or five rebounds, stole the ball once, and blocked two shots in a scrimmage against the first team." I do remember that I felt good about the way it was going — and was thinking, if I'd been this good last year and had played more, I might have a chance to make it now. It wasn't just dunking in warm-ups. I'd put on about fifteen pounds and was now about 190, stronger, a better all-around player. I remember twice, in that early scrimmage against the first team, pulling up and hitting jump shots, off the fast break, from the head of the key. But I was also handling the ball better, playing better defense, even setting picks and boxing out and doing the little things I hadn't always done before.

Why did I always look good in tryouts, and then fade as the days and weeks went on? That's what had happened last year, and I knew deep down it would happen again if I stuck around long enough — that the weaknesses that were still there would again be exposed. But I didn't stick around after the second week. Before practice one day Coach Smith called Bill Vick and me in again and said we had looked good but that the numbers were against us. As we went out of his office, he called me back and said, if I wanted, I could continue to practice with the team, and if someone got hurt might be able to dress for home games — but I still wouldn't make the traveling squad. In any case, he said, I could go on and practice that afternoon. Why not? I thought. With the missiles in Cuba, the world could be blown up any minute. What better place to be than Woollen Gym?

Thirty-five years later, when Coach Smith inscribed for me a copy of his memoir, *A Coach's Life*, he wrote, "With your athletic ability, I should have tried to persuade you to be a member of the varsity on the 1962–63 team." Kind of him, I thought, but I remembered that afternoon three, nearly four, decades earlier, and knew what he had known: there was no way I could ever have been a . . . *contributor*. As I had walked to the locker room that afternoon I had weighed what he said about continuing to practice with the team. I was tempted, but even I was realistic enough to know I would never play much if any at all — might not ever dress at home. And the next year would probably be the same. I knew it wouldn't be worth it.

But I would enjoy this last practice, knowing it was the last. I got a lot of playing time in the scrimmage that afternoon, and again, like the week before, I was hitting — two or three outside shots, a couple of inside jumpers. It was a clocked scrimmage and I was in the game as the time went under two minutes. Someone on my team, I've forgotten who, got a rebound on the other end, and passed out to Peppy Callahan, a reserve guard from Long Island, who broke to the middle and passed to me on the left wing. Two or three players were already back on defense and the middle was clogged, but I liked it outside. I pulled up and let fly with what I knew would be my last shot as a Tar Heel. It felt good, but it was just short and to the left. Off the rim. It would have made no difference, of course, if it had gone in. But there—on a late October afternoon with sunlight filtering through the windows and the world about to come to an end over Cuba—I sure wish it had.

7

Romance of the Book

So it was all over, at least in the sense that playing basketball had any future to it. For about a year, it seems, after my Tar Heel stint, I possessed no particular identity, or at least not one I can look back on with any pride — ex-jock, gym rat, who wore his old Tar Baby practice jersey on the court and his freshman letter jacket around campus, still sometimes getting nods from strangers who were so hoop-crazy they remembered even last year's freshman bench-sitters. I joined an intramural team and played the kind of loosely structured game Coach Smith would have never allowed — jumping and shooting and blocking shots, forgetting all about such niceties as position defense and setting picks and boxing out. But since I weighed more and had learned the art of throwing elbows from the best, I played a more physical game now. Soft, hell — I wish Lyles could see me now.

On afternoons when I wasn't playing intramurals I sought out pickup games, shirts vs. skins, and for the first time I found myself playing a lot with and against black players, some UNC students, some former and current

high school and college players from Chapel Hill and
Durham. Though it's hard to generalize, the black guys
played what was then coming to be known as playground
ball but in fact was the way of the future—more freewheeling, more creative, with a premium on dazzling
moves and no-look passes, on leaping and quickness and,
generally, more physical play. Though Jim Crow was not
yet dead in Chapel Hill—a quarter of downtown busi-
nesses were still segregated in 1962—all seemed equal on
the court. Though we mixed it up under the basket, I
don't recall any fights, any encounters, even any tension.

For a while I thought about trying some other sport,
some less competitive one, on the varsity level, but nothing quite fit. The closest I came was after an intramural
track and field meet when the varsity track coach, who'd
been on hand, asked me to come by his office. At the
meet I'd won the high jump, despite never having competed in the event in my life. With no technique at all, just
leaping and tucking my knees to the side, I had cleared
5'8."

When I went by to talk with him, Coach Hilton asked
if I'd like to try the broad jump. Why not the high jump,
I asked, since that's what I seemed to do best. He said my
build wasn't right for it—I weighed about 190, too much
for high-jumping on a 6'3" frame—but that with training
I could be a broad jumper. He was wrong. I worked out
for a week or so with one of his assistants but was unimpressive from the beginning. Although I could jump I
wasn't particularly fast; thus I couldn't build up enough
speed approaching the takeoff board to get any real ac-
celeration. Where was the athleticism Coach Smith had

talked about? In fact, it was never fully there—that is, I
wasn't fast and I wasn't particularly strong. I was a sort
of an athletic *idiot savant*, a jumping curiosity, and I had
good reflexes—perfect for basketball, but not of great
use in anything else.

So, I finally concluded: a failure in basketball, a failure
in track, and there was nothing left. I hung around the
student union for a while, making a reputation for myself
as a Ping-Pong champion—the reach and reflexes helped
there—but intramural Ping-Pong champ didn't quite have
the ring of Carolina basketball player, so I soon gave that
up. Then, I decided, if I couldn't compete in sports at the
major college level, I could at least write about them—
which had been my professional goal, insofar as I had
one, in coming to Chapel Hill in the first place. So I de-
clared myself a journalism major, went to the offices of
the *Daily Tar Heel,* and signed on as a sportswriter. The
Tar Heel, I knew, had a long and storied tradition—its ed-
itors ranging from Thomas Wolfe (1919–1920) to Charles
Kuralt (1954–1955), Ed Yoder (1955–1956), and Jonathan Yardley (1960–1961)—and it had won numerous
national awards for excellence. Sportswriting was hardly
what its reputation rested on—that calling might seem to
lack the requisite high seriousness—but it was about all I
knew and all I could write about. Hadn't Grantland Rice
been a legendary American writer? And hadn't James
Reston begun as a sportswriter, and Tom Wicker, and
numerous other giants of American journalism? So a
sportswriter I would be.

My first assignment for the *Tar Heel* was to cover track
and field, and I figured I could handle that: it had been

Bannister vs. Landy's "mile of the century" in 1954, after all, that had captivated me as fully as anything had before basketball passion set in. I went by to talk with Coach Hilton—whose interest in me as a broad jumper had now waned—and he filled me in on the hurdles and the shot put and other events I knew little about. Within a week or two, in the early spring of 1963, I was getting bylines in the *Tar Heel* and finding that sportswriting allowed more license than any other assignment on the newspaper: although the subject might not be socially significant, there was the *illusion* of transcendent importance as well as the opportunity to make your prose stand up and perform. Alas, I went in too heavily for performance, going overboard for alliteration, laying the adjectives on especially thick. I remember a headline story I wrote about the biggest track meet of the year, against Duke, when I waxed particularly eloquent about Duke's discuss thrower, "diminutive Dave Gesswein." I thought "diminutive" meant large and powerful—it *sounded* large and powerful—and it got through the *Tar Heel* copy desk with no trouble. It was only when I sent the article home and my father read it that I discovered, to the contrary, that "diminutive" meant "extremely small."

Through my *Tar Heel* reporting I landed a job that summer as a sportswriting intern on the Winston-Salem *Journal and Sentinel.* That meant I would get to work with Frank Spencer, the dean of North Carolina sportswriters, a stocky, gruff, cigar-chewing veteran who bore an uncanny resemblance to Spencer Tracy. I also thought I would work with Bob Cole, the author of the piece "King Arthur and His Court" that had awakened me to writing as a high school junior. In fact I worked with neither, though I shared the same large desk in the sports wing of the newsroom. Mainly I covered Winston-Salem's bowling leagues, dominated by a local legend named Ski Kwiatkowski, and, on Saturday nights, stock car races at Bowman Gray Stadium. This was not the big time: Bowman Gray had only a quarter-mile track, and the drivers rarely exceeded seventy or eighty miles per hour even on straight stretches. The average track speed was more like fifty. But Bowman Gray was legendary—it had been, about fifteen years earlier, essentially the birthplace of NASCAR—and fans flocked from all over northwest North Carolina to see the successors to those earlier giants, Curtis Turner, Lee Petty, Tim and Fonty Flock. My story in the Sunday paper was always given big play.

As the summer went on, I got tired of bowling and stock car racing. The other interns, in the news and editorial departments, seemed to command much more respect around the newspaper. They also seemed to know a lot more. My ignorance, both intellectual and social, was especially exposed one night when Wallace Carroll, editor and publisher of the *Journal and Sentinel* as well as former deputy head of the Washington bureau of the *New York Times*, invited several of us to his home for dinner. I got off to a bad start when artichokes were served: I had no idea what they were or what to do with them—I assumed they were to be eaten, but I didn't know in what manner—and I got by only by sneaking glances at how others were handling them. After that, conversation turned to a couple of books that had recently appeared,

J. D. Salinger's *Franny and Zooey* and Walker Percy's *The Moviegoer,* neither of which I had read or even heard of. I said nothing.

When I returned to Chapel Hill in September, I vowed to master both artichokes and contemporary literature. Sportswriting would no longer do it. Neither would journalism as a major. I went over to the Arts and Sciences office and changed my major to English, which the undergraduates I respected most—even those heading for med school—had chosen. My mother had been an English major, after all, and my aunt an English professor: maybe it, if nothing else academic, was in the blood. It would also spruce up my ex-jock image, not to mention do something for what I'd come to perceive, at least for that moment—after having rubbed shoulders with Atlantans and Charlotteans and Raleighites, not to mention Long Islanders—as the cultural liability of being from the North Carolina hills.

So in September 1963, at age twenty, I finally discovered books—for the wrong reasons, maybe, but at least I discovered them, even *embraced* them as something that could be pursued outside the classroom. It was in the classroom, though, that I first felt their impact. Chapel Hill in those days had a number of stars in American literature, but the first upper-level English class I chose, the American novel, was taught by a nontenured instructor, a freshly minted Ph.D. named Julian D. Mason (the D for DOG, a friend of mine said, for all the D's he gave). Julian Mason wasn't flashy, wasn't spellbinding, but what he had to say about literature—and its ties to society, history, and region—I remember to this day, as well as the twelve novels on his reading list, and the exact order in which we read them, from *The Scarlet Letter* to *The Grapes of Wrath*.

One way to read novels for the newly converted and thus not fully initiated is to read them in intensely personal terms, and that's precisely what I did. Sherwood Anderson's *Winesburg, Ohio* I saw as the story of my hometown — all its characters, its eccentrics — shifted five hundred miles northward. Sinclair Lewis's *Babbitt* caught my town's newer spirit — civic boosterism, business opportunism and club-joining, back-slapping conformity — and Thomas Wolfe's *Look Homeward, Angel*, set in western North Carolina, captured the flavor of the hill people I knew.

In all the novels I read I saw people I knew, or maybe it was the other way around. In my paperback edition of Henry James's *Portrait of a Lady* — the edition, nearly forty years later, I still use when I teach the novel — I see jotted in the margins, next to descriptions of James's heroine Isabel Archer, the words "just like Celestine" and "Celestine would do that." Celestine was a sometime girlfriend, or rather a kind of inaccessible ideal, refined and reserved in a way that had great appeal, though she often seemed about as remote to me as Isabel Archer was to her suitors in James's novel. Ensconced in an exclusive woman's college in Virginia, she had never been able to come down for a game during my freshman year, and thus had never seen me play as a Tar Baby: that, I had hoped at the time, would have broken down the reserve, would have sealed the deal. But the deal had remained unsealed, thwarted a second time in November 1963 — just about the time, in fact, that I was reading *Portrait of a*

Lady — when Kennedy was assassinated and the Duke-Carolina football game, which she was coming down for, was postponed. Celestine was only one of many characters I recognized as I read James and Mark Twain and Faulkner. Every afternoon, that time formerly given to basketball, I made my way to the reading room of the student union, an elegant room with fine rugs on the floor and overstuffed chairs and soft lighting and portraits on the walls, and stayed two or three hours, losing myself in another time and place.

I realized how far behind I was in reading good books, the kind my parents had on their shelves but I had never touched, and how much catching up I had to do. But the idea of catching up was exciting — nearly as exciting as basketball had been and, in a curious way, almost as competitive. I read in Wolfe's *Look Homeward, Angel* the description of his autobiographical hero prowling the stacks of the Carolina library fifty years before, pulling books off the shelves and devouring them. Though no one could approach the Faustian appetites of Wolfe, I would try.

One book I found, by the contemporary novelist Peter DeVries, had a character ridiculing another character as "a man who had never heard of Mencken," and I thought I'd better look up this Mencken and see why it was important to have heard of him. Pulling his *Prejudices* off the shelf, I turned to his essay on the South, "The Sahara of the Bozart," and in it I found prose such as I had never encountered: "One thinks of the interstellar spaces, of the colossal reaches of the now mythical ether. Nearly the whole of Europe could be lost in that stupendous region

of fat farms, shoddy cities, and paralyzed cerebrums. . . .
In all that gargantuan paradise of the fourth-rate there is
not a single picture-gallery worth going into, or a single
orchestra capable of playing the nine symphonies of
Beethoven, or a single opera-house . . ." and so on. I
wasn't sure everything Mencken said was completely
true, but that wasn't the point. It was *how* he had said it
that launched me on a study of this American Voltaire,
one that would later cause me to write three books on the
man, though I could never have imagined that at the
time.

H. L. Mencken was writing about the South of the
1920s, but the more I read the more I thought of my own
South of the 1960s. Maybe not a Sahara artistically any
more — I had read enough now to know that Faulkner
and Wolfe and Robert Penn Warren and Flannery O'Connor had taken care of that — but still Mencken's "Bible
Belt," his backward and savage South. Every month
speakers were coming to Chapel Hill — C. Vann Wood-
ward, Ralph Ellison, Malcolm X, Will Campbell, and
many others — but I hadn't been to hear them. Now I
missed no speakers who came to Memorial Hall, not even
staunch segregationist Governor Ross Barnett of Mississippi, invited for balance and greeted by a front row of
black students who proceeded to walk out when he tried
to convince them that some of his best friends were
Negroes, including, he said, "an ole darkey I go bird-
huntin' with."

I looked south, to Mississippi and Barnett, to Alabama
and George Wallace, to South Carolina and Strom Thur-
mond — and, finally, I looked where I should have been

looking all along, to Chapel Hill itself. Chapel Hill, of course, was accustomed to examining the rest of the South—it was proud of its reputation as the most liberal spot in Dixie—but it wasn't in the habit of examining itself, and neither was I accustomed to viewing it very critically. It wasn't that I was completely unaware of what had been going on there—the marches, the sit-ins—during the two and a half years I had been on campus. It's just that I hadn't paid much attention.

I recall, in fact, a Saturday afternoon basketball game, preceding the varsity game, my freshman year in which—as we took the court against someone, I've forgotten who—we noticed that the stands weren't full and that something seemed to be going on. Outside, a civil rights demonstration had moved from downtown to Woollen Gym, some of the fans were delayed getting in, and I remember being a little irritated that we couldn't get on with the game. As I looked back, even from a vantage point two years later, I realized a lot of ironies had been at play in that, not the least of which was that the *real* game, both for the future of southern athletics and for the future of the South, was going on outside; and another of which was that, if the civil rights revolution had been carried out not after 1962 but before, I and a lot of my white teammates might not have been playing college ball at all, at least not in a Carolina uniform.

All this was finally sinking in by my junior year, although it should have sunk in long before. The Chapel Hill phase of the civil rights movement, which had begun in 1961, had continued throughout my freshman and sophomore years. Two of the leaders were my classmates,

John Dunne, an honors graduate of Choate and recipient of one of Carolina's top academic scholarships, and Pat Cusick, the son of conservative Alabamians. Both withstood beatings and were arrested numerous times for sitting in at segregated restaurants, and both ended up serving one-year prison terms. My sophomore psychology instructor, Al Amon, another sit-in leader, had also been beaten; he had suffered the additional indignity—while sitting, or rather lying, in—of having the wife of a local restauranteur squat over him and urinate on his head.

So I knew what was going on and altogether approved of the sit-ins (even, at least after my freshman year, if they invaded the sacred precincts of Woollen Gym), though I did very little myself to be a part of them. My older sister, a Carolina graduate who had moved to Tennessee after graduation, had helped to integrate a downtown Nashville restaurant, and my parents certainly supported her activities. And I myself, reading the newspapers, looking at Huntley-Brinkley, and hearing the multitude of speakers who came to Chapel Hill, was becoming increasingly aware of the high stakes in the southern drama.

How could you help it, looking south to Oxford, Mississippi, and seeing the hatred and violence at the admission of James Meredith to Ole Miss? How could you help it if, as many of us did, you tuned in Channel 5 in Raleigh every night at 6:25 and heard WRAL editorialist Jesse Helms rage against "liberals, Communists and Nigras," particularly those at Chapel Hill? And how could you help it if, as we did on two occasions, you went to

Klan rallies in cow pastures near Durham, saw the hoods and the burning cross and heard the racist vitriol? I saw and heard all this, but did little but observe. Only once, my junior year, did I join a civil rights march, and that was a rather tame affair down Franklin Street.

But I was becoming *aware*, which is much more than could have been said for me a year before. The spring of my junior year I started reading a lot of Faulkner—first one of his easy novels, *Intruder in the Dust*, which dealt with racial violence in the Deep South, then the much richer and more difficult *Absalom, Absalom!*—another exploration of racial intrigue in Mississippi. I also read a couple of Deep South autobiographies, as different as they could be in their points of view—William Alexander Percy's *Lanterns on the Levee*, the nostalgic recollections of a southern planter, and Richard Wright's *Black Boy*, the bitter story of a black sharecropper's son. What Faulkner, Percy, and Wright had in common was that they all were from Mississippi, a place I had never been in my life but one that seemed a whole lot more exotic, and certainly more violent, than my own upper South (the "Shallow South," as John Shelton Reed was later to call it, as opposed to the Deep South). That impression was reinforced when I read that northern college students were planning to come south in the summer of 1964—into "the Heart of Darkness," one piece put it—to register black citizens to vote. It was to grow even stronger when, early that summer, I read that three civil rights workers were missing in Mississippi and then, six weeks later, that Andrew Goodman, Michael Schwerner, and James Chaney had been found buried in an earthen dam in Neshoba County.

It is to that spring and summer that I can trace the origins of what I would later call my bad case of Mississippi envy. That is, if I were going to be a writer of some sort and I planned to write about the South, why couldn't I have been born in the Heart of Darkness, with all its action and angst, and not in the hills of northwest North Carolina, 90 percent white, devoid (at least it seemed to me at the time) of a rich and violent history and a tragic sense (apparently I forgot my own boyhood street), altogether lacking a Gothic sensibility and devoid of mystique. The Mississippi envy only increased when I later read Willie Morris's *North Toward Home,* Anne Moody's *Coming of Age in Mississippi,* and any number of other memoirs. In fact, for the next couple of decades it was to seem that every literate child, white or black, who had grown up in Mississippi turned out an account of his or her tortured heritage.

During the spring of 1964, finally awakened to the larger world and indulging in a romantic yearning to be at least a small part of it, I had clipped from the *Raleigh News and Observer* a passage from Oliver Wendell Holmes, Jr., and placed it, self-importantly, over my desk: "A man should share the action and passion of his times at peril of being judged not to have lived." That summons to a cult of experience should have meant, the summer of 1964, heading for Mississippi and freedom summer and the high drama unfolding there, but either a certain caution or a misunderstanding about where that action and passion really lay drove me in another direction: while northern students came south to Mississippi, I headed west, to Washington and Oregon and California, to work in canneries with Mexican migrants. My friends and I had been reading Faulkner, but we had also been reading Steinbeck and Kerouac and Kesey and we heard there were cannery jobs to be had in the West—not in Steinbeck's Monterrey sardine canneries but in the pea canneries of eastern Oregon and Washington and in fruit canneries near San Jose.

So five of us drove west in my old 1957 Pontiac, and worked in a series of canneries on the West Coast—although that summer, for me, was to have a southern theme as well. As we drove through Wisconsin, Minnesota, the Dakotas, Montana, and Idaho, and then settled into a migrant camp near Walla Walla, I was reading not Steinbeck and Kerouac but a southern book, one that I was coming to believe was at least as good as Faulkner— W. J. Cash's *The Mind of the South*. All of us were reading as we drove across the plains, sometimes even the driver, and I hardly remember North Dakota passing by.

Cash was that good, and he worked even better than Faulkner for me because he was writing largely about *my* South—the upcountry and piedmont South of the Carolinas, the textile belt. But he also changed my mind about an aristocratic Deep South: the origins of most southern "aristocrats" were lowly, he insisted (which I should have already known from reading Faulkner), and in fact they weren't aristocrats at all. In a similar manner Cash demythologized the entire South. As the summer went on, as I read about Goodman and Schwerner and Chaney and other southern atrocities, I kept turning back to Cash for explanation. I later learned that this shy, somewhat eccentric North Carolina newspaperman, who committed suicide shortly after his book appeared, didn't have all the answers—he had his own set of blinders—but he told the truth mainly, and he could write about as well as Mencken.

We read many other books that summer—we had a lot of spare time on our twelve-hour graveyard shifts in a series of pea and peach canneries—and not all of them dealt with the South. I recently found a letter I'd written to my parents in late July in which I listed nineteen novels I'd read in the previous two months, with a lot of Steinbeck and Hemingway in the mix. And life in the Green Giant labor camp was fascinating enough in itself that reading might seem a sort of second-hand knowledge. Most of the occupants were migrants up from Mexico, and after working in the pea fields and canneries of Oregon and Washington, they would head—as many of the college students in the camp also would—to California for the fruit harvest. I had never before seen a Mexican to my knowledge, was full of the usual Anglo stereotypes, and spoke no Spanish at all. Although the migrants were friendly enough to me, I can't say I came to know them very well in the two weeks we spent in the camp before finding a cheap motel near our cannery. But that didn't keep me from posing as instant expert on migrants and migrant camps and writing a series of articles that I sent back to my old newspaper, the *Winston-Salem Journal.*

But mostly that summer, my mind was on the South. I

read not only Cash and Faulkner but also Wolfe and Welty and O'Connor and Ellison, I read and saw the news from the Deep South, and there, in those small towns of Washington and Oregon and California, twenty-five hundred miles away from the southern drama, my own southernness announced itself to me more forcefully than it ever had back in Dixie. Heading back across country in late August, this time taking the southern route, I experienced a much greater thrill in approaching Mississippi than I had in approaching California for the first time. Though we were driving a car with North Carolina plates and we all had southern accents more or less, we felt apprehensive enough that we all shaved the beards we'd grown that summer — though, in fact, we were probably as safe in Mississippi as we would have been in the outer reaches of eastern North Carolina.

When I got back, it was for my senior year at Chapel Hill, and I was ready to write about the South — and about the 1964 Johnson-Goldwater presidential race, in which I strongly supported LBJ. I signed on as an occasional columnist for the *Daily Tar Heel*, appearing at times on the same page as the *Tar Heel*'s sole conservative columnist, Armistead Maupin, at the time a strong Jesse Helms supporter who was still a few years away from coming out and making a name as one of America's leading gay writers. But journalism, at least for the present, was not what I principally wanted. I wanted to keep reading, I decided, and that meant graduate school, but my grades were so mediocre in English — I had never made an A — that I had no hope of being admitted to any self-respecting graduate program. The problem, I later realized, was that I had no idea how to approach literature as *art;* I approached it only as social history. When I got a question on a Romantics exam about Keats's imagery, I turned it into a discussion of the Industrial Revolution. When I got a question about Coleridge's aesthetics, I found a way to talk about the Lake District. I took a degree from one of the nation's finest English departments without knowing the meaning of a metaphor.

But as mediocre as I was in English, I had made A's in all my history courses, which gave me a glimmer of hope. I was not even a history minor, but I did have the grades, at least in the only four courses I had taken, and along with high scores on my graduate record exams, that got me admitted to Duke for their master's program. My plan, as I had told their department head when he interviewed me, was to become an interpretative journalist (even if I didn't know exactly what that meant), and I needed the background in American social and intellectual history. In any case, I wound up the following fall in Durham on the campus of the Tar Heels' legendary adversaries—and basketball came back into the picture.

It had not disappeared altogether, of course, during the previous two or three years when I was discovering books. But the Tar Heels had continued to have mediocre seasons, this despite the earlier prediction by *Sports Illustrated* that the arrival of Billy Cunningham and other recruits would land the Heels back among the nation's best. Cunningham had indeed gone on to stardom as a three-time All-American, but his New York sidekick Jay

Neary had left school after his freshman year, and most of the other recruits from the early '60s had not panned out as expected. So, four years into Dean Smith's reign, there was still nothing, at least on the record, to presage greatness.

Duke, on the other hand, was riding very high, and my admission to that august institution brought me tickets to Blue Devil games. In fact, for the next two years, I may have been the only Tar Heel on earth whose second-favorite team was the Devils. I had all those Tuttles from my mother's family who had worn Duke blue, after all, though in football and track, never basketball, and besides, the basketball Devils were in the nation's top five to begin the 1965–1966 season.

The peak of my brief Duke allegiance, heretical as it may seem and secondary though it was, came during December 1966 when top-ranked UCLA came to North Carolina for two games against the Blue Devils, the first to be played in Durham on a Friday night, the next the following night in Charlotte. UCLA was the defending national champion, and the Devils were primed. In fact, the scene in Duke Indoor Stadium that night was probably as frantic as any that already aged arena had ever seen, save on certain occasions when the hated Tar Heels had come to town. It was almost nice to be for Duke for once, and with Jack Marin and Mike Lewis leading the way, they dominated the Bruins, 82–66, in Durham, then 94–75 the next night in Charlotte. The next week they were number one in the country and would go on to the Final Four that March.

In fact, during those years, like my last couple of years in Chapel Hill, I managed to maintain a healthy interest in—but not my earlier (and later) obsession with—basketball. That, I am told, is the way it should be: the ideal of the average fan, one who could actually *enjoy* a game without living and dying with it, as had been my approach to hoops as a child and, alas, was later to be again. But during that period an obsession with books continued to take the place of basketball—all those great works of American social and intellectual history by Henry Steele Commager and Vernon Louis Parrington and Henry Nash Smith and William Leuchtenberg. What did *they* care about basketball?

The romance of reading, then, as well as falling in love in a more conventional sense, did it for me—that is, removed basketball from the center of my life for a time. As hard as it is now to imagine, at age twenty-three I found myself, on a balmy evening in March—an evening Duke and a suddenly resurgent Carolina were playing for the Atlantic Coast Conference tournament championship—on a picnic by a brook with the woman I was later to marry, occasionally checking the car radio for the progress of the game but not really caring exactly what happened. It was, in fact, a momentous evening I missed, one during which the Tar Heels, behind Bob Lewis and Larry Miller, ended the Dukies' eight-year run, winning 92–79 and launching their own twenty-year reign in the ACC. And what was I doing but having a picnic on a blanket by a brook? It didn't come to me then but it did later in what I came to call Eros' Law: that it is impossible, at least in one's youth, to be crazily, actively, in love, and also, at the same time, care with all your heart about the outcome of a particular basketball game. The two passions must stem from an identical core, and they simply can't coexist.

But that is in the early, crazy phase of love. With marriage, which came not long after that, basketball came to assume its rightful place — although still not in the absolutely obsessive fashion of earlier and later years. In fact, the period between ages twenty and thirty is the one time I may have lived something approaching a balanced, normal life as a fan, tuning in games and caring about the outcome but not agonizing every waking moment over possible recruits and starting lineups and injury reports. As my father would have said, for once I was getting my priorities straight.

After I finished a master's degree at Duke, I took a one-year job teaching English, not history, at an all-black school, Livingstone College, in Salisbury, North Carolina. It was my first teaching experience, and it couldn't have been a better one. The school, affiliated with the AME Zion Church and headed by a member of a prominent black family in Salisbury, reminded me somewhat of the black college, modeled on Tuskegee, in Ralph Ellison's *Invisible Man* — a school that put a premium on decorum and propriety, a more Victorian place than any white school I'd ever seen — although my impression of Livingstone was more favorable than Ellison's of his college. I particularly admired the senior African American professors, men and women in their fifties and sixties who had labored for years with inadequate facilities, low salaries, and a deep commitment to public service.

At Livingstone, basketball took more of my time than it had since my sophomore year at Carolina, but at least my interest, this time, was largely professional and social: many of my students were good players, a lot of them from Detroit and Cleveland, and, for me, playing was another form of keeping office hours. Like a lot of white guys in that era, I was coming to associate, too closely probably, blacks and basketball. When I assigned paper topics under the "comparison and contrast" section of the freshman English syllabus, I gave "Wilt vs. Russell: Who Is Better? — and Why?" as one of the possible topics. (Bill Russell was the choice, two to one.) When once I lectured on classicism and romanticism in literature, I gave as an example the white Bill Bradley (eighteenth-century classical style — methodical, all calculation and practice) versus the black Cazzie Russell (a vintage romantic, the Blake of the hardwood). Obviously, I hadn't come quite as far up from racial stereotyping as I'd thought.

After the year at Livingstone I knew I wanted to teach, or at least to go back and get a Ph.D. in literature and then see what would happen after that. And I knew I wanted to focus on the literature of the American South. In 1967 Dixie was no longer quite at the center of the nation's attention — Vietnam now held that position — but my interest in what W. J. Cash called the mind of the South, and particularly that tortured corner of its mind that dwelled on race, was as strong as ever. Still, during the waning days of the civil rights movement, I had largely sat on the sidelines, marching only once or twice and never risking anything. Perhaps that was why, in part, I had gone to Livingstone to teach. Salisbury was the home of the Grand Wizard of the Ku Klux Klan in North Carolina, and I felt a thrill at the slightest possibility that I was courting danger—though in fact, for a white southerner in 1967, teaching at a black college, even in a Klan haven, was probably about as hazardous as serving as register of deeds or selling crop insurance.

If I wasn't fully sharing the action and passion of my time, I was at least observing and writing about it. On Palm Sunday 1966, while visiting my sister in Atlanta, we went to Martin Luther King's church, Ebenezer Baptist, and heard King, Daddy King, Andrew Young, and most of the Southern Christian Leadership Council hold forth from the pulpit. The hymns were the same ones I knew from back home—"Just As I Am" and "All Hail the Power of Jesus' Name"—but one wizened old man in the congregation put the sermon in contemporary terms. "Why did they crucify him?" asked Wyatt Tee Walker, the primary preacher that day. "Because he was colored," the old man shouted.

With race and the southern mystique on my mind—with a year's cramming for the Graduate Record Exam in English and a newly discovered knowledge of the meaning of a metaphor—I applied for graduate study in English at Chapel Hill, reputed to be the best place to ponder the mysteries of the southern mind. This time, having used Duke as a kind of prep school, I was admitted. There was good reason to be motivated: the young woman I had just married was a much better literature student than I was, but, trapped in an era just before the gender rules changed for both of us, she had decided to give up her Ph.D. study at Duke to teach honors English in high school and see me through to a Carolina degree. The term gender guilt had not yet been invented, but I sure felt it.

That and the feeling that I still had so much catching up to do—that all these other Chapel Hill graduate students had been reading good books since they were ten and I had just begun to read at twenty—meant that, from 1967 to 1969, there was almost no time at all to be a basketball fan. These were the years that Carolina, led by All-Americans Larry Miller and Charlie Scott, went to three straight Final Fours, but I hardly went to a game. I thought it had to be all books or all basketball; I could focus on only one thing at a time. In fact, the competitive atmosphere of graduate study duplicated to a great extent what I had earlier felt in basketball—wanting to write the best papers, get the best grades, finish the degree faster than anyone else—except this time, at least for a while, I think I wanted it more than I ever had in basketball. Sitting in my carrel, deep within the bowels of Wilson Library, writing my dissertation, was the same sort of exquisite solitude I had found in my backyard as a kid playing basketball—living in my own world, creating my own narrative.

Except, of course, it didn't have to be all books or all basketball, a realization that sank in one day as I walked behind three stars of American literature—Louis Rubin, Hugh Holman, and Richard Harter Fogle—as they made their way to Lenoir Hall for lunch. They were discussing not Faulkner's prose style or Ellison's use of the mask but instead Charlie Scott's jump shot and Dick Grubar's grace under pressure. I was astounded: these were professors, and they were excited about basketball. They were also, in the manner of later professors I have known, applying the same critical skills to their discussion of basketball that, an hour or so before in their classrooms, they had been applying to Mark Twain and Eudora Welty.

In fact, their discussion shouldn't have surprised me. My parents' Duke faculty friends, Wes and Lola Williams—who had become my intellectual mentors when I first discovered books—were also basketball fans, or at least Wes was. And, later, when I was doing research in the Fugitive papers at Vanderbilt, I found that those letters exchanged between John Crowe Ransom and Donald Davidson in any given September or October were full of references to the fortunes of the then-proud football Commodores. So I shouldn't have been surprised when I heard Louis Rubin talk to Hugh Holman about jump shooting, but it was a shock of recognition: I could be a professor and a basketball fan too.

But not for a while, not until I had read a lot more books. The only thing I had to do with basketball in graduate school was, occasionally, to play it, and as much for the camaraderie and exercise as for competition, although in fact the English Bards—so the graduate team was named—ended up being one of the best teams I'd ever played on. We had two starters who had played on big-time freshman teams, a 6'6" center who had started three years at Davidson College, and a point guard—one Charlie Altieri—whose tough New York Catholic school background prepared him well for both the rigors of intramural competition and the world of literary theory, in which he later was to excel. The graduate and professional intramural league had never seen anything like it—a team made up of *literature* students that was beating everyone in sight. Altieri dished out the assists, I hit the jumpers, and Joe Milner controlled the boards. In a league of nearly a hundred teams, the Bards reached the tournament finals, beating doctors and chemists and historians along the way, only to lose by six to a bunch of law students, led by my old freshman teammate Pud Hassell.

That was the end of it for me, really the end this time, the last organized or even semi-organized game I would ever play. The next fall, on a gray Sunday afternoon, in a rough pickup game on the same Woollen Gym court where I had dunked my way onto the freshman team seven years earlier, I went up for a rebound, came down, and was hit from the side just as I planted my left leg. The pain was so bad I thought it had to be a broken leg, but, for a basketball future, it may have been even worse—a torn anterior cruciate ligament. Even today, that usually means a year out of action for a varsity athlete. In 1969, particularly when you were twenty-six and couldn't devote every minute to surgery and rehabilitation, it was a veritable basketball death sentence. After three months on crutches and another couple of months limping, I knew it was over. Or it should have been.

But, of course, I had to give it one more brief try. Rather than teaching freshman composition while writing my dissertation as most other graduate students did, I had decided to go to work as an editorial writer for the *Winston-Salem Journal*—though both the *Journal* publisher, Wallace Carroll, and I should have known a twenty-six-year-old is too young to write editorials. While in Winston, after laying off basketball for a year and feeling that the knee had improved a little, I decided to play in a benefit game that was to include a few former ACC players. I remember the point guard for the other team was Billy Packer, former Wake Forest star who was later to become CBS's basketball guru, and I remember I got in the game toward the middle of the first half. Within a minute, on the left baseline, I jumped to block a shot and came down on the bad leg. Again, it bent sideways, and again I had to be hauled off the court. And, again, crutches for several months.

I stayed at the *Journal* for a year. I caught on fast enough to the trick of writing editorials—reading up for a few hours on a selected or assigned topic and then posing as instant expert in a six-hundred-word essay for the next day's paper—and I found we could write about almost anything we wanted. (Except tobacco: in Winston-Salem that required far more delicacy than editorials about nuclear proliferation.) If a particular editorial didn't reflect precisely the *Journal*'s position, it would usually appear as a signed column—which was even better. During the campus uprisings of 1970, particularly after the massacre at Kent State, it was also decided that I, fresh off a university campus, should be the designated writer on student dissent. That and much else was heady stuff— our staff won a Pulitzer Prize that year for its writing on environmental issues—but all the while I felt like something of a fraud. On a great number of topics—Eastern Europe, the Middle East, South Africa—I was always pretending to know more than I really did, and I always felt I would be found out. Besides, after the paper had gotten some favorable mail (largely from the Wake Forest professoriat) for a lengthy, rather abstruse piece I had written on Kent State, Wallace Carroll sat me down and said all that high-minded prose was well and good, but if I was really going to stick in this business, I had to "learn to write for the man in Waughtown."

Mr. Carroll was right: the trouble with liberals like me in 1970 was that we didn't really know much about the man, or woman, in Waughtown, the large white working-class district of Winston-Salem. But that — my ignorance about Waughtown — isn't why I left the *Journal* after a year. I left because I wanted to write longer things, books, and that meant, if I were to have any means of financial support, I had to get a job teaching in college. I left too because my wife and I had run into an Englishwoman whose husband, the chief administrator of the coal-mining borough of Barnsley, found us jobs teaching high school for a year in Yorkshire. Figuring we would never get to England, at least on a paying basis, any other way — and we had long been taken with the idea of England — we jumped at the chance and wound up in a coal-begrimed place once called by a BBC commentator "the ugliest town in England." It had plenty of competition in Yorkshire's heavily industrial West Riding — including, ten miles away, Wakefield, which I had assumed would be the charming pre–Industrial Revolution town of Oliver Goldsmith's eighteenth-century novel but turned out to be a dark, grim city of a hundred thousand.

Being in Barnsley also meant, for the first time in my life, complete basketball withdrawal — for in England, in 1970, no one had ever heard of hoop. In Spain, maybe, a little, they had, and in the old Soviet Union. But not in England—except, briefly, I was told, five or six years earlier, when Bill Bradley had come to Oxford as a Rhodes Scholar and had drawn a little attention in some circles. But news of Bradley and basketball had never penetrated Barnsley. "Isn't that similar to netball?" one of the other teachers asked me when I once mentioned basketball. The teacher had in mind the least strenuous, least athletic of games played by the scholars of the Barnsley Girls Grammar School in their gray woolen uniforms. Margaret Thatcher, in her own girls grammar school in nearby Grantham, no doubt had once been a netball stalwart.

In the previous five or six years, when I had weaned myself from a complete dependence on basketball, I figured that I had left behind a certain phase, that I had now grown up and that games really didn't matter that much to me any more. But in England, when winter came, I sat on long cold nights in the cottage we'd rented in the green countryside (for there was a green countryside, though often reconstructed on the top of slag heaps), stoking a coal fire for whatever warmth we could generate against the winds coming off the moors, and realized I wanted to know more than anything else what was going on just then with the Tar Heels and Blue Devils and Wolfpack.

But there was no way to find out: the English sports pages had not a word about American college basketball, not a score, and the *International Herald-Tribune* (which couldn't be found in Barnsley anyway) rarely did either. I realized then what should have been obvious but what I had never considered before—that sport is, after all, the most provincial of interests. As a friend back in America wrote me, after I had complained that I couldn't find a single mention of basketball in English newspapers: "You shouldn't be surprised. To those Brits, ACC is nothing but the village in Italy where St. Francis was born."

Only once in all my stay in England did I see a basketball hoop, and just why it was where it was still mystifies me. We were driving back from London one Sunday afternoon, taking the A1 up through the flat, green farmland of Lincolnshire, when suddenly there it was—a basketball goal, somewhat but not completely rusty, nailed to a primitive backboard that rested at the top of a pole, approximately ten feet in the air. It was in a field with the grass cut fairly short, but there was not in front of the goal, as there always is in front of American goals similarly situated on poles or barns or garages, an area where all the grass has been worn off. There was just the hoop itself, with no house within a hundred yards of it, no basketball in sight, no boy or girl.

I have no idea how the goal had gotten there, in this remote part of Lincolnshire, only a few miles, in fact, from the home of William Bradford and the original Pilgrims who had left England for America in 1620. Had some English schoolboy discovered the game and badgered his father to find and nail up a hoop? Had Bill Bradley, in his days at Oxford, passed this way and, like Johnny Appleseed, left his calling card? Had some expatriate American, otherwise enamored of this sceptered isle, realized there was one thing England couldn't give him and sought to remedy that? Or had some descendant of the original Pilgrims wandered back to the land of his origins, bringing a hoop with him? I would never know, of course, but I would wonder about it for years.

Except for this lone hoop in a field about twenty miles from Lincoln Cathedral, I saw no evidence that the English had ever heard of basketball. But, in fact, I realized, I was just as ignorant of what mattered most, in the world of sport, to *them*—what *they* turned out in masses to see, what they agonized over in front of the telly, what they sat discussing with dead earnestness in pubs while having a pint. When we first arrived, in August 1970, the World Cup had just been concluded, and I *thought* I was told that England had won it, defeating West Germany in what sounded like a replay of the Second World War. In fact, until very recently, I still thought England had won it. Everyone in the working-class pub I frequented in Barnsley, lilting away in that musical Yorkshire accent it took me a while to understand, could talk of nothing else but football and, I thought they said, England's victory in the World Cup.

In fact—now I discover, thirty-five years later—England had not won at all: Brazil had defeated Italy in the 1970 finals, and England had been *beaten* in the quarter-finals by West Germany. How could I have misunderstood? Because the Yorkshiremen in the White Hart who told me had been talking not about 1970 but about the *1966* World Cup finals, in which England had indeed beaten West Germany in London's Wembley Stadium before ninety-seven thousand fans—and four years later they were still exulting in the victory. This says a lot not only about the difficulty of the working-class Yorkshire accent to a newly arrived Yankee and about the devotion of the

working-class English to football—that they had been rejoicing over a victory from years in the past as if it had
just happened. It also says a great deal about my own ignorance. Understand that in those pre–global village days,
with no CNN and no ESPN, I had never even *heard* of
the World Cup, and I barely knew that football meant
soccer. I had never heard of Manchester United and
Sheffield Wednesday, Arsenal and Tottenham and West
Ham, or scores such as "nil-nil," and I wondered about
the grammatical construction of the headline on the sports
page: "Barnsley win."

But in England, particularly working-class England,
real men, even real women, knew that football—soccer—
was what mattered, and I soon got into the spirit of the
game as well, going every Saturday afternoon with a couple of Yorkshire friends to the local pitch, standing on the
terrace, swaying back and forth, and seeing Division 3
Barnsley take on Huddersfield and Bradford and Wakefield and Doncaster. I was amazed by the *all-business* nature of soccer as it was played in England, at least in grim
industrial Yorkshire, that land of the dark, satanic mills—
no marching bands and cheerleaders and halftime shows,
no cute nicknames and mascots, no announcement of
starting lineups or other ceremonial trappings, no dressing up as fans still did in America, at least the American
South, at that time for football and basketball. At least in
1971, in Yorkshire, there was just tough, nonstop football, running and passing and shooting, and, at the Barnsley
pitch, five or six thousand strong—almost all men, many
of them after a week in the pits—standing on the terrace
(I knew no one who sat), pouring out a series of unintel-

ligible chants in a rhythmic hum, a sort of Yorkshire glossolalia.

Grimly—it being Barnsley—they would accept defeat, then move on to the White Hart and other pubs to drown their sorrows. Maybe in London and Manchester and Birmingham soccer fans rioted after losing, but not in Barnsley. In a hard land, even soccer—played in all sorts of weather, most varieties foul and cold—was a hard business. Compared to that, basketball—netball!—*did* seem to be for sissies, an innocuous frivolity, presided over by schoolmarms, conducted at recess for the grammar school girls, and sometimes boys, of the West Riding.

I survived the hoopless Barnsley winter, depending on week-old letters to tell me what was going on with the Heels and the Devils—transatlantic calls being too expensive in those days—and then learning, about the time the daffodils came out, that UCLA had won still another NCAA title. (Keeping up with recruiting was even harder: when I left America, I thought Carolina had just landed the top high school prospect in the country, Tom McMillen; when I returned, I discovered he had changed his mind at the last minute and gone to Maryland. And all of England had managed without that news.) To that winter without hoops, I think, I can attribute my renewed obsession for the game.

But access to basketball, at least that brand of it invested with North Carolina life-and-death intensity, improved little when I returned to the United States. The following year I took a teaching job in another place, Alabama, that lacked the requisite reverence for the game. Tuscaloosa, nearly as much as Barnsley, lived and died with football, except of course the Crimson Tide variety was played with pads and helmet and a ball of a different shape. Bear Bryant was coach, and as they said in Alabama there were three seasons—football, spring football, and talking all summer long about the previous year's Bama-Auburn game. The reverence for the Bear was such that when he died a decade later, the folks lined the streets of Tuscaloosa as the hearse passed by, then lined the overpasses and sections of the interstate to Birmingham where he was to be buried. It was not unlike the masses who had turned out to line the roads for the martyred Lincoln on the way to Springfield. Or, to keep it in Bryant's own country, not unlike the throng of poor and plain southerners who poured out of the piney woods in Faulkner's story "The Bear" to pay homage to another legendary creature—another bear—who had long dominated and finally had fallen.

So the Deep South was given to rule by pigskin. Southeastern Conference basketball meant Kentucky, and not much else. Although Alabama had a new coliseum and was starting to build a respectable team—thanks in large part to racial integration, which arrived on the basketball team my first year there—real fan interest was still a few years away. And, in 1973, interest in hoops beyond the SEC was almost nonexistent. Carolina and Duke could be playing each other, an event of transcendent importance, and the late-night sports news on Tuscaloosa and Birmingham stations wouldn't even have the score. This was just before ESPN, remember, and before the nation's saturation with ACC basketball—which later reached such a point that one notable Pennsylvania recruit was to say he had thought the ACC was a television program, not a conference. But in 1973, it took a phone call back to North Carolina the next day to find out what had happened the night before. I might as well have been in Yorkshire.

This hunger for basketball news—as well as a sort of messianic drive to spread the gospel of basketball, especially its ACC variety, in the Heart of Dixie—completed the task, begun in England, of resurrecting the obsessed basketball self that had lain dormant in me for several years. And, my second year in Alabama, the renewed hoop obsession did one other thing: it made me want to play again. I had not touched a basketball, except perhaps to shoot HORSE a time or two, since I reinjured my knee in Winston-Salem three years earlier. But the knee had seemed to improve. I had hiked the Yorkshire Dales and the Pennines and the Lake District, and I had even begun to play a little tennis, with a brace my orthopedist recommended.

When I hit Alabama what happened to me is what happens to many ex-jocks who hadn't really been that good but had once played a little bit, somewhere, near the upper levels of their sport. That is, they suffer an inflation of reputation. I know a man who, back in the 1960s, had ridden the bench for a certain ACC team, but I recently heard him described as a former all-conference player. My reputation was hardly inflated to that degree—and I was always honest in describing my extremely modest accomplishments. But rumors spread, especially among graduate students who, like me back in Chapel Hill, could not believe that a professor, whose face was now always in a book, could have once been known for something else. Thus I was talked and tempted into taking the floor one winter night with Bama's graduate English team as they went up against a team of chemists. I stuck on my knee brace, got out my old Converses, and took the court.

I lasted only five minutes, and this time I didn't even have to jump, or get hit by anyone, to tear up my knee again. I just planted my left leg to push off for a jump shot — and collapsed in a heap, the pain much worse than it had been in Winston-Salem. This time just going back on crutches for a couple of months wouldn't take care of it. When summer came I went to Duke Hospital and had surgery, not for the purpose of playing basketball again but just so I would have a serviceable knee for life. The surgical resident had heard from a friend of mine, whose knee had also passed under his knife, that I'd played a little basketball for Carolina, a very little, but that was enough for him. I can still picture his devilish grin and remember his words as I went under: "Ah, the chance to cut on a Carolina knee."

This time, playing basketball was over for good. Three or four years after the surgery I finally got back to being able to run and play a little tennis, wearing a much better brace that covered a third of my left leg, but I would never again be tempted to play basketball, other than a game of HORSE. At age thirty-two I was completely washed up. But that was only as far as playing. On the other basketball front — whether *because* I was washed up, or because I found myself down in Alabama, cut off from Carolina basketball and moved by an impulse to enlighten the natives; or whether I was so affected by my recent divorce, the resulting off-and-on brief separation from my four-year-old daughter, and the vacuum that created in my life—whatever the reason, my life as a fan would become even more intense. It would remain so for the dozen more years I would stay in the Deep South, and become no less tortured when, in 1989, I finally returned to Chapel Hill.

8

Second Childhood

"As I get older, the tyranny that football exerts over my life, and therefore over the lives of people around me, is less reasonable and less attractive."

— Nick Hornby, *Fever Pitch*

Hornby was talking about English soccer, not American college basketball, but he got it just right: an unbalanced devotion to a game that might be appealing in a ten-year-old kid, even amusing in a twenty-year-old college student, is downright ridiculous in a man of late middle age. It's especially ridiculous when the man in question — on a rational level — disapproves of much of what the game represents: the big money, the hypocrisy, the somewhat euphemistic talk of "student-athletes" and the "academic side" (shouldn't that be a university's *only* side?), and so forth. I've taught at the University of North Carolina for sixteen years now, and in that time I've had a thousand or so students pass through my junior-senior American literature courses — but not one of them has been a scholarship basketball (or football) player. And North Carolina and Duke are among the *most* academically respectable programs in big-time basketball, a reputation, relatively speaking, that is well deserved: they refuse to accept less academically qualified junior college transfers (and, in former days, refused to take academically deficient Proposition 48 athletes), their players "go to class" (another college hoopspeak cliché), and over the past three or four decades they have "graduated their players" (still another) at almost a 90 percent clip, far exceeding the national average. Yet, I think it's pretty safe to say that not a single men's basketball player currently on scholarship at North Carolina or Duke, based on those institutions' average entrance exam scores, would be there if he didn't play basketball.

So I see the hypocrisy, and I also hate the sportscasters' hype: "giving 110 percent" and "stepping up" and "leaving it all on the floor" and so forth. I've even found myself at times — again, on the rational level — finding the whole idea of basketball a little absurd. Football, by contrast, makes sense, drawing its logic from military conflict — two sides lining up and charging at each other with the object of moving deeply into the other's territory. But *dribbling* a ball (the very word suggests infancy), trying to put it in a small hoop, all the while wearing short pants and T-shirts — isn't there something infantile about all that? If civilization were done over again, we might go a million years without anyone thinking it up.

In fact, I often do think that way in November, and even through Christmas and the bowl games, but after that I begin to take refuge in a sort of Coleridgean suspension of disbelief. The season requires it. After all, can you imagine an average weeknight in February without college basketball on TV? It's at that point in the year that the subconscious takes over: I begin to dream about basketball—once or twice a week—and in about half the dreams I still have a good knee (not to mention youth). In most of the dreams I am trying out for some team—it *can't* be the Carolina varsity again, all these years later, but I don't know what else it might be—and I'm hitting my shots and leaping prodigiously, but in the dream I'm always afraid I'll soon be found out for the mediocrity I am. In still other dreams I've already torn up my knee and know any minute I'm going to hurt it again, but I can't stop playing.

That's *sick*, but at least I can blame it on my subconscious. What's even sicker is that, when I'm awake, I cultivate this kind of thing. Like Updike's Rabbit Angstrom, I pass kids playing three-on-three on an outdoor goal, and I have the urge to stop and join the game. (You don't have to be a has-been to have this urge: when he took his sabbatical to play minor-league baseball in Birmingham, Michael Jordan once passed a boy shooting in his driveway and *did* stop his car, get out, and join the boy.) At halftime, in Carolina games at the Dean Dome in front of twenty-two thousand fans, when some kid whose ticket has been chosen is called down to the floor with a chance to win a thousand dollars or a new car—or whatever is offered: the prize doesn't matter—by hitting first a layup, then a free throw, then a three-pointer, and finally a shot from midcourt . . . I want to be that kid.

As I drive the three hours to my mountain cabin in late

spring, still suffering from post-NCAA angst, I find myself projecting Carolina's starting lineup for the next two years; I find myself coming up with the Heels' all-time underachieving team; I wonder why almost all the great college basketball teams (UCLA, Kentucky, Carolina, Duke, Kansas) wear blue, and almost all the great college football teams wear red or orange; I try to think of all the teams whose nicknames do not end in "s," starting with the Fighting Irish and Crimson Tide and Wolfpack and then getting to the tough ones; I trace lines of basketball influence (Phog Allen to Dean Smith to Larry Brown and Roy Williams) the way other English professors trace prose style in Twain to Hemingway to Raymond Carver.

The year before last, winding along the Blue Ridge Parkway in early May, to all appearances taking in the rhododendron and wild azaleas newly in bloom, I broke a thirty-minute silence and startled my girlfriend Barbara with the cryptic words, "If he'd only called a time out." And the season, remember, had been over for a month. I can't leave it behind even at work. In an American lit seminar, I sometimes think of myself as a sort of verbal point guard, spreading the questions around, getting them all involved—getting *assists*. And, on the computer, on those occasions when the writing's going well, I think of myself as, well, a shooting guard when he can't miss—unconscious, in a zone.

Even more—since this has turned into a sort of ugly confessional—I might as well say that I half resent those colleagues of mine who still have good knees, those without the zipper surgical scars up the inside of their legs, who come back to their offices from the gym after lunch glistening with sweat and beaming over just having taken some graduate student one on one. A poet friend, in his mid-fifties, is still in particularly fine form. A skilled point guard, he even writes poems on "the weave, the trap, the backdoor pass," the lob so perfect that his teammate can "in a single motion . . . catch and finger roll it in." He can still execute that perfect lob. I, on the other hand, am reduced to HORSE, a game that involves only shooting. Although HORSE has a certain attraction of its own—a psychological game-playing, a guise of not taking the contest seriously, no matter how much you really want to win—it still isn't the real thing. It's not really basketball.

I go further than envy and even cultivate an uncharitable habit of judging other men my age, at least those I knew as boys or younger men, on the basis of whether, at that earlier time, they had good jump shots or not. I still remember what their jump shots *looked* like, even thirty or forty years later—and if someone had a particularly ungainly one, or did not have one at all, I have to fight the tendency to judge him harshly, as being of no worth, no matter that since then he may have written a prize-winning novel or acquired his own company or made a hundred million dollars or won high elective office. (I wonder if my friend Win, captain of the 1964 Andover team and possessed of a classic jump shot, still sees his old roommate George Bush—who had none, and thus occupied the end of the bench—in that light.) *Why* I do that, a shrink would say, is perfectly obvious: in those earlier days I was clearly inadequate in all other respects—

in music, art, electronics, social graces, and eloquence — and it was for self-protection that I came to judge others altogether by my basketball standard.

But I am no jock-sniff, understand, one who idolizes athletes, who ventures out between classes to the spot outside the library where Sean and Jawad and Rashad hold court, receiving admirers with a lofty grace. I'm not even an outwardly obsessive *fan*, one who shows up to greet them when the Heels return from a transcendent victory, who frequents Internet chat rooms, not even one who wears a baby blue Carolina sweatshirt to games and joins in the wave and the "TAR . . . HEELS" cheers. My problem, I fear, is a more serious one, driven by a kind of rigid moral absolutism, a desire to make the outer world conform to my own inner world — the same kind of thinking, I'm sure, that drives assassins and serial killers to do what they do. My grand, abstract view of the universe has the Tar Heels astride the basketball world (as they have been for much of my life, through all those record years of twenty-win seasons and Sweet Sixteens) and a Democrat in the White House (there too, conditioning plays a part: one *was* there the first nine years of my life).

I'm not the only one who views the world this way. Recently I was discussing post–Dean Smith recruiting lapses in the Tar Heel program with the gracious seventy-year-old southern lady whose office is next to mine — another believer in the Chapel Hill trinity of basketball, barbecue, and liberal politics — and suddenly she got a steely look in her eye. "Somebody's got to *pay*," she said, and I understood: the moral order of *her* universe had been violated too, the Heels had descended, if only for a transitory moment, into mediocrity, and all had to be made right. I also think of a notable novelist I know, a South Carolina native, who has had a lifetime addiction to Clemson Tiger basketball. Clemson Tiger *football* would be one thing—they are always respectable and sometimes very good—but Clemson basketball is quite another: almost always last in the ACC. Yet, though a graduate of loftier universities and currently a teacher in another institution that always has a nationally ranked basketball team, he lives and dies with the Tigers, although reality has never conformed, not once, to his inner universe.

They both have it bad, but I have it much worse. I consider the consequences of my affliction. An optimist generally—the sort who assumes, if he is driving on a remote road in Nevada in a car almost out of gas, that he'll come upon a station any minute—when it comes to basketball, I am utterly pessimistic. That was not the case when I played; there too I was an optimist. On the line with the clock running down, I always assumed I'd hit. So the pessimism as a fan is caused, no doubt, by my total lack of control (or even the *illusion* of control) over the situation.

All this affects the way I approach Tar Heel games. Seeing a tense game live, at the Dean Dome, is painful but not as painful as all the other options: at least, if the Heels lose to the Deacs or the Terps or the Wolfpack, twenty-two thousand people all around me—dressed in Carolina blue, even if I'm not—feel my pain. Seeing a game on television, at least a game you have a reasonable chance to lose, is unbearable. You can't see the whole picture: again, you don't have even the illusion of control. But hearing a game on the radio is worst of all. You are at the mercy of announcers who are also Tar Heel partisans and tend to see the game, at least their first draft of it, the way they want to see it.

The pain of seeing—and the prohibition on hearing—makes for problems, particularly when I encounter those who believe a basketball game, and receiving its results, is a social occasion. Numerous times I've invented excuses to avoid seeing games—important ones, that is, that the Heels are in—in the presence of other people. Totally out are dinners or parties of any sort organized around seeing a big game. Sports bars are even worse: you can't see clearly, you can't hear, you are in the presence of infidels who come to the altar of basketball without the requisite high seriousness. People are actually *eating* while watching McCants take a jumper that will spell victory or defeat. Would you eat in church?

The only way to see a game on TV, if you must, is at home (and, again, let me point out, lest you think I'm obsessed, that I speak only of games guaranteed to be close and those in which defeat, if it comes, will be especially painful), and you have to lay in your stores in advance, spiritually speaking. My partner, Barbara, knows basketball well—her father was a college play-by-play man—and she also possesses both the requisite seriousness and passion for the game, but even at that I usually retreat to another television in another part of the house, and there sit, in splendid isolation, preparing myself for what is to come, ordering my universe—again, the sort of focused, single-minded vision that assassins must have. No alco-

hol at hand, only water, and a keen awareness of space —
room on all sides to jerk and twist.

Even with such preparation, things often do not work
out. I remember a Saturday afternoon game once, when
my daughter was about five; she woke up from a nap and
appeared in the door of the den where I was watching the
Heels struggle to hold on to a two-point lead over the
Runnin' Rebels in the final minute of the national semifinals. She had shown early promise as a Tar Heel fan. By
age three — down there in Alabama — she knew all the
Carolina songs, and often burst out with her favorite,
which she called "the bread song." (I'm a Tar Heel born,
I'm a Tar Heel bred. And when I die, I'm a Tar Heel
dead.") Once, when she and her mother and I, along with
her maternal grandmother from Cleveland, were taking a
long car trip and Jane had been entertaining us with
North Carolina songs, her exasperated grandmother burst
out, "Doesn't she know any Ohio songs?" So Janey had
early priorities right, had potential as a Tar Heel fan, but
conduct such as mine during that Carolina-UNLV game
undoubtedly took its toll. She had no idea the minefield
she was entering that afternoon: I bolted upright (she
later said), swung my arms, and emphatically motioned
her out of the room. Sacred space had obviously been
violated.

A few years later, over spring break, some time after
Jane's mother and I had been divorced, Carolina and
Syracuse were battling down to the wire in the Eastern
regional finals when her mother stopped by to pick her
up. My daughter, having altogether rejected basketball
by now, was back in her room reading, so she suffered no

abuse this time. But her mother later said that, standing at the front door, she heard my voice—loud, angry, obviously disturbed—and took a full five minutes to realize it was the TV, not our daughter, that I was yelling at.

Not only the game itself but the entire day of a really big game—an NCAA regional final or, the holy of holies, the Final Four—is ruined for normal living. I become a virtual Cotton Mather, seeing signs everywhere, finding meaning in the invisible world. I make a bet with myself over whether an approaching car will reach a particular road marker before I do, or whether the next car I come upon will have a 3 in its rear license plate, with the outcome of the game at stake. I find other ways, some altogether shameful, to cope with pregame angst. I rarely bet on basketball, but when I do—and the game is crucial and guaranteed to be close—I have to confess, I usually bet *against* the Heels. Not a large bet, only ten dollars or so, but it is a psychological investment, a sort of loss insurance, which assures me that I win either way—either I'm right or I'm happy. Such a practice would obviously get me banned from the Big Leagues, and may even jeopardize my tenure in Chapel Hill, but there it is.

All the above assumes, of course, that I can control my game environment, where and how I see the action, and by and large I can. But not always. The worst of situations is when, for professional reasons, I have to be out of town at a conference of some sort and am required to show up at a reception or party at which—I know in advance—a television will be tuned to some particularly important game involving the Heels. The hosts, I'm sure, do this as a *favor* to sports fans, who can check on the score while they talk postmodernism or semiotics or the chances of landing a chair at Brandeis. But the effect is anything but positive.

I recall, nearly a quarter century ago, when I was in my first teaching job but had my eye, down the line, on a particularly attractive position at another university that would come open in a year or two. I was scheduled to meet, at a Saturday afternoon party, the man who would be most influential in any subsequent hiring, and who also happened to be an eminent editor as well as one of the leading figures in American literary studies. This was in November, football season not basketball, but the football Heels had their best team in three decades and would head to a major bowl if they beat the Maryland Terps and won the ACC championship that afternoon. I had hoped a television set wouldn't be in the room, but there it was, and soon I found myself sitting in front of it, tuning out everything but the announcer's voice.

We were down by two in the fourth quarter, with time running out, when I felt a tap on my shoulder, and after ignoring it for a second or two I looked up and confronted the Editor. I jumped up, shook hands, and mumbled a few words, all the while with one eye on the television, grimacing and jerking as I followed the action. Soon, seeing my mind was elsewhere, the Editor excused himself, and I went back to seeing the game come to a bitter end with the Heels just out of field-goal range. I had blown it both ways. I *knew what I had done* — not only had I been unspeakably rude to a kind and gracious gentleman but I had undoubtedly ruined my professional future. I jumped up and ran across the room, trying to find him again, but he had gone. Addiction had done me in. And this had been *football:* how much more churlish would I have been if the ball had been round?

So why not give it up? Addictions can be beaten, after all. The smoker, more and more these days, gives up his Camels, the drinker his Jim Beam, the foodaholic his nightly quart of chocolate ice cream. In fact, I found out years later from the Editor himself, the eminent figure I had ignored that Saturday afternoon in Atlanta, that he himself had once given up just such an addiction, which might explain why he later seemed to forgive me for my rudeness. He had, in his early days as a professor, been a committed University of Texas football fan, but he had found that it was interfering with his work and his sleep—one night, in particular, after a painful Longhorn loss, he lay awake all night—so he ditched it, went cold turkey and, he said, no longer even followed football. *That* was a reasonable course, I had to admit—especially since, in my own case, the addiction involved so much more pain than pleasure, the agony at losing being so much more intense than the thrill of winning. And even if you won a very big game (unless it was the NCAA finals, and even that, as we shall see, presents problems), another big one, another potential disaster, always loomed. It was not a matter of if your heart would be broken. It was a matter of when.

Acknowledging all this, a few years ago—when the Heels were suffering their worst season in a century—I did make an attempt to get out. Not go cold turkey, not give up all interest in hoop, but more of a halfway covenant, as the Puritans would have called it. I would stop buying season tickets to Carolina home games (for, briefly, things were so bad that they were even losing at home) and I would *tape* all games home and away. I would set the VCR for each game, get some necessary reading done during the action, and then, casually, almost as an afterthought, tune in afterward to see how things had come out. I would be approaching basketball the way my father had, receiving the final score, calmly, dispassionately, *maturely*, and then turning in. No jerking and twitching, no grotesque rituals: if the Heels lost, I would feel pain only once, when I heard the score.

All that sounded reasonable enough and it almost worked for a while, particularly because the Heels were so hapless that single year, 2001–2002, that after a time, nothing—an ACC title, an NCAA bid, finally, god forbid, even a lowly postseason NIT bid—was really at stake. I even took a kind of morbid interest in the whole thing: if they're going to have their first losing season in half a century, I thought, they might as well do it in as dramatic a fashion as possible. The plan was fine for that one year, then, but the next season the Heels brought in three of the nation's top eight recruits, won the preseason NIT at Madison Square Garden, and were a threat to win any game they played from then on out—though they lost a lot of maddeningly close ones. I continued the taping that year, but now with a certain edge. Barbara, the devoted but sane Tar Heel fan (though she taught at N.C. State, she had never fully bonded with the basketball Wolfpack), remained in the den to see the game live, and I slinked off to my study, equipped with white noise maker and the Norton Anthology.

Barbara understood fully (we had spent hours working out the ground rules) that she could make all the noise she wanted, could cheer and moan and cuss, because my sound machine would drown out all that. She would let me know when halftime came, and then she'd cut the volume down so I could sneak into the kitchen for food or drink. At the end of the game, she'd come into the study to tell me it was over—though she operated under strict instructions to give no hint as to the outcome of the game, to say no words at all, to make no gesture or facial expression that would give it away. No comment, in fact, on *any*thing, even if unrelated to basketball, since some bit of knowledge might be encrypted in her words.

The plan was good, in theory. But problems began to arise. First, there in my study, reading was impossible. I was looking at words from Faulkner but could picture only air balls from Jackie Manuel. Second, phone calls: after a couple at timeouts or halftime from friends with highly excitable tones, wanting to talk about Sean May's post moves or Quentin Thomas's turnovers, I realized I would have to take the phone off the hook at some point during the first half and leave it off until I had not only received but digested the final score. And there was the problem of how, and when, to receive the score. At first, as originally planned, I got it all at once—Barbara volunteered to run the VCR to the place that had the final score on the tape, at which point she would leave the room. Then I would plop down in my chair in front of the TV, steel myself for what was to come, tell myself that this was not life and death after all, only basketball (though I can't imagine the death row inmate in *his* chair, waiting for the switch to be thrown, would have felt much more anxiety), hit the remote and take it head on.

After a few games, I decided, receiving the score in this manner was too much of a jolt at once. I began to rewind the entire game, going back to the beginning, and then see it in segments. If the Heels took an early lead, and continued to lead, I let it run its course. (Obviously, in doing it this way—not really seeing it live—I was relinquishing that illusion of control that many fans, and once I among them, feel they have over the game.) If the Heels fell behind, I fast forwarded to see if I could find a place in the game when they were back on top. In a close game—and keep in mind it was only those games that had a strong possibility of being close that I taped—I crept toward the end, often stopping with ten or fifteen seconds left, with the Heels up or down by one or two and the outcome in the balance. Again, I went through the mantra ("this isn't life or death; its outcome has no real importance to my life . . ."), and then took a deep breath, plunged into the electronic abyss, and the devil fetch the hindmost.

Getting the outcome this way, of course, I received it in an altogether solitary manner. If it had been a night game, by the time I received the final score the rest of the house was silent. Barbara had long since gone to sleep, and so had the rest of the world, including anyone I could call to gloat or commiserate. So I would sit there alone, on an average cold Wednesday night in February, seeing the coals die in the fireplace, taking in other scores from across the nation, seeing all the country as a sort of giant basketball electoral map, so many red teams and blue teams falling into place on a single evening—feeling a certain sense of elation or gloom with nearly every score, since one of the results of being a truly committed fan is that you have formed an opinion, either love 'em or hate 'em, of nearly every team across the land. And after that, if the Heels had won but I had skipped parts of the game, I would replay the entire thing—and if they'd lost, also replay the entire thing, backtracking and fast-forwarding, seeing just what had gone wrong. One of the advantages of taping, I'd earlier thought, is that I wouldn't waste so much *time* on basketball—I'd get the score, see a few highlights, and that would be it—but in fact I found myself sitting late into the night involved in a film session worthy of Jim Boeheim or Rick Pitino.

I said this would be a confessional, and I fear it has been. A genial, good-natured, low-key sort most of the time, slow to anger and hesitant to give offense, I become a thoroughly unpleasant person, surly and self-absorbed, petty and vindictive, when an important game is on the line. So, a confessional it is, though I'm still not sure you really believe it. Once, more than twenty years ago on a weekend when the ACC tournament was being played in suburban D.C., I wrote an op-ed page piece for the *Washington Star* on my basketball addiction, and I got letters from a few readers saying it was one of the funniest pieces they'd ever read. *Funniest?* In fact, I had been dead serious, not kidding at all. And I am serious now. Certain games—not most, only a very few—stick with me forever. Some losses are left behind the next week (almost never the next day), most by the next month (unless they result in an unfortunate NCAA seeding), some linger into the summer, and a select few gnaw at me for years.

I still wake up some mornings thinking about the loss to Marquette in the 1977 NCAA finals, a game in which the Heels, crippled with injuries to Walter Davis, Tommy LaGarde, and All-American Phil Ford, stormed from behind to take the lead in the second half, only to go into Dean Smith's infamous Four Corners delay game, lose momentum, and, then, the game itself. Or I find myself driving through some desolate stretch of the Carolina Piedmont pondering the day still known on Tobacco Road as Black Sunday—March 11, 1979—when I broke away from a wedding reception in Alabama to discover that Carolina *and* Duke, both overwhelming favorites, had lost back-to-back in the Eastern Regionals to what were supposed to be two patsies, Penn and St. John's. Or I find myself hiking along the Blue Ridge or paddling the New River agonizing over the loss in the 1981 finals to Indiana, the Monday night of the day Reagan was shot, still wondering whether the near death of a president, and the day-long indecision over whether to go on and play the game or not, fired up the right-wing Bobby Knight and stirred some sort of residual guilt in the left-leaning Dean Smith.

But the games I remember most are those which were indeed of great consequence in the larger world of sport but were also, in some fashion, interwoven with what I might call, for want of a better term, the minimalist drama of my life. A dozen or so stick with me, but I will summon up only five or six, and not all of them defeats, in fact some of them glorious victories.

To wit:

Carolina-Alabama, March 13, 1976. The Heels were 25–3 on the season, loaded with talent — All-Americans Phil Ford and Mitch Kupchak, along with future Olympians Walter Davis and Tommy LaGarde — and occupying their customary perch in the nation's top five. They were heavy favorites over Alabama, a football school after all, but Phil Ford had injured his knee, and, besides that, the Heels were overconfident. This game meant so much because, as I mentioned earlier, I had landed at Alabama three years before as a professor and also saw myself as something of an emissary of basketball, coming from the heart of hoops civilization, the ACC, to the hinterlands of the Deep South. I was out to spread the gospel, driven by a kind of noblesse oblige of the hardwood.

The game came on a Saturday, at the beginning of spring break, and my wife and I had taken a place for a long weekend on Dauphin Island, off the Gulf coast of Alabama. I have always been a fair-weather beachgoer, and March in Alabama — no matter what they may think in Michigan and Nebraska and Montana — is often anything but fair weather. But my wife and I, having withstood a series of illnesses, injuries, and family traumas over the past year or so, had decided our marriage needed a boost, so we left our two-and-a-half-year-old daughter with my parents, who had driven down from North Carolina. Saturday dawned bleak and rainy and, after taking a long walk on a cold, dreary beach — I limping along on my gimpy knee (which maybe, at some level, I associated with Phil Ford's), still not recovered from the surgery eight months before — we settled in the room to view the

Heels and the Tide, there being no VCRs in those days to postpone the pain. Sure enough, the Heels came out sluggish, not ready to play, and Ford's knee made him completely ineffective. Bama, led by one of its first black players, Leon Douglass, thoroughly outplayed the ACC prima donnas and won by fifteen.

I have always associated that beach weekend with the end of my marriage, a marriage that had once been so awfully good I had, a decade before, almost forgotten basketball for a while, or at least put it in its proper place. The marriage didn't end there on Dauphin Island—in fact, it didn't end for another year and a half—and I can hardly hold Phil Ford and Mitch Kupchak responsible for its demise. But the game was the first of many things that went wrong that weekend—cold and stormy weather, no good restaurants to be found, a general homesickness for the Tar Heel state—and, an opportunity lost, maybe it was something of a beginning of the end. I left there with a deep sadness, which was hard to define, but I'm sure—petty as it might appear in the larger scheme of things—that the Heels' defeat played some part in creating that mood. Besides, having spent three years touting the ACC, having dismissed Bama as a football school, what was I to say to the boys back in Tuscaloosa?

Carolina-Alabama, March 19, 1982, and Carolina-Georgetown, March 29, 1982. This year the Heels were indisputably the nation's best, from November (when the starters appeared on the cover of *Sports Illustrated*, all except Michael Jordan, because Coach Smith didn't publicize freshmen) through mid-March, when they entered the Eastern Regionals with a record of 27 and 2. But it

was also the year I had missed seeing them altogether because I was off teaching in England for a second time and
getting the results a few days late in the *International
Herald Tribune*. Basketball coverage in England had improved little since my previous stay there eleven years
earlier. Now, though you could on rare occasions see
English basketball on television, the patient tone of the
play-by-play man suggested the Brits had a long way to
go. "He was above the iron," I heard the announcer mar-
vel one early spring day as I watched the Cup finals from
Wembley. "The iron, remember, is ten feet off the floor."
So the English weren't there yet, and had absolutely no
interest in the fate of the Tar Heels.

By mid-March, just before the Eastern Regionals, I
couldn't take it any more; I booked a flight to Atlanta,
where my sister lived, for the Saturday and Monday of
Final Four weekend. That involved a display of optimism
I have always tried to avoid at all costs: planning to be
within television range of the Final Four presupposed
that Carolina would *be* in the Final Four, and to plan it—
such would usually be my reasoning—would jinx it. To
be honest, that wasn't the only reason for the flight. My
daughter, now living with her mother in New Orleans,
planned to come to England for a few weeks with me
when her school year ended in late May, but I missed her
very much and didn't want to wait that long to see her. So
she would fly to Atlanta and we would have a few days
together, which would (I wonder if she would have come
if she had known, remembering her past encounters with
hoop madness) coincide with the Final Four.

But to reach the Final Four the Heels had to win three

games in the Eastern Regionals, and by the time of the regional semifinals—as fate would have it, against Alabama again—I couldn't stand the tension, the not knowing. I had heard that I might be able to tune in Armed Services Radio from my remote outpost in the North of England. So on a Friday night, in my ancient and drafty house in Kingston upon Hull, I set my alarm for 2 a.m., went downstairs to an iron-cold kitchen, turned on the radio, and moved the dial back and forth until an unmistakable midwestern accent, on a frequency blowing across the North Sea from Germany, told me the NCAA Eastern Regional semifinals were on the air.

No one else in Yorkshire cared. Outside, the winds blew up from the River Humber to the south, down from the moors and dales to the north, and the rain beat against the window. I sat by my radio, squeezing the dial to bring back the fading voice, while the dock workers and shopkeepers of Hull slept. Arsenal or West Ham or Manchester United—for *these* they might get up in the middle of the night; or, this being rugby territory, for their adored Hull Kingston Rovers. But no one knew, or cared, that Villanova was playing Memphis State that night, that Kansas State was playing Boston College, that Georgetown was playing Oregon State—and that the Heels were taking on the Tide for the right to go to the Eastern Regional finals. Sport, it came to me again, was the most provincial of passions—one of the deepest, the most enduring, but the most local.

The Heels won that game, 74–69, though I had to struggle for every minute of it, since—in addition to the usual problems with narrative reliability on the radio—

the announcer's voice kept fading in and out, the winds and waves of the North Sea keeping me from the truth. I turned in about 5 a.m., knowing that, if Carolina could knock off Villanova on Sunday (which they did, in an easier game), I would be seeing the Heels next weekend after all. Both my daughter and I reached Atlanta that next Friday, and we spent a full day and night doing non-basketball things. I reveled in seeing her but I also went around with the foreboding of a condemned man, knowing that the Heels would take on Houston with Clyde Drexler and Akeem Olajuwon late Saturday afternoon and I would have to get my game face on. At 3:30 on Saturday Jane took a book to her bedroom and I found a place on my sister's couch, prepared myself to be as civil as possible since it was my sister's house after all (and I had suffered a couple of painful TV defeats there before), and vowed not to scream and rant and cuss beyond an acceptable limit. It was a tight one, but the Heels took the Cougars 68–63, and now I could go back to enjoying life for another day with my daughter before she flew back to New Orleans late Sunday and the Heels took on George-town—also in New Orleans, as it happened—Monday night.

That game is still billed as one of several contenders for national Game of the Century: the Heels, with All-Americans Sam Perkins and James Worthy and All-World-To-Be Michael Jordan, versus the Hoyas, with Patrick Ewing, the most intimidating college center since Wilt, and Sleepy Floyd and a couple of other future NBAers. One can say that sports mean nothing, and that may be true, but *if* sport has meaning this particular game was one of the most meaningful ever. For Dean Smith it meant everything — perhaps the nation's top active coach (with the possible exception of Bobby Knight), with seven Final Fours and three national championship games (this was the fourth) to his credit, but still not a national title. For me it meant more than any game in exactly a quarter century, since March 1957 when the Heels had beaten Kansas and Wilt. And the scenario was eerily reminiscent of that earlier game: the Heels ranked number one in the country but a slight underdog in the title game because they were facing a truly dominant big man and a team that had been annihilating its opponents.

I remember every moment of the Carolina-Georgetown game, Ewing's goaltending in the beginning, intended to intimidate, and Worthy's full-court drives and swooping dunks. With thirty-two seconds left and Georgetown leading 62–61, Coach Smith called time out. As my sister and I sat there waiting, I kept shouting obnoxiously, "Jordan, Jordan" — meaning get the ball to Jordan. Wanting Michael Jordan to take the last shot might seem obvious now, since he was to become the greatest player in the history of the game, but in 1982 he was a skinny, baby-faced freshman and, at most, the third-best Carolina player. The best, Worthy, had already scored 28 points and seemed to be the likely go-to guy, but Jordan had played well the second half and looked confident. And it *was* Jordan, as all hoop historians now know, who took and hit the jumper, the sixteen-footer from the left wing with seventeen seconds left — the jumper billed in newspapers and magazines for weeks as "the shot heard round the world" (though it had hardly penetrated the remote reaches of Hull, as I discovered when I got back).

After Jordan hit, the Hoyas' Fred Brown, in another moment destined to live in television archives, mistakenly passed the ball to the Heels' Worthy, and that was it. Coach Smith had his national championship, the legend of Michael Jordan was born, and as I flew into London's Heathrow early on a cold gray Wednesday morning, daffodils in bloom in fields below, I felt just like I had twenty-five years before when the Heels had beaten Kansas for their first NCAA title. I was thirty-eight now, and should have had graver concerns, but all I could think about was Jordan's jumper, the flick of the wrist, the flight of the ball. Though it would occupy only a few paragraphs in the *International Herald Trib* and escape mention altogether in the *Times*, the *Guardian*, and the *Spectator*—and could never be appreciated by a sporting public whose primary game did not allow the use of hands—to me it had been a thing of transcendent beauty.

Carolina-Michigan, April 5, 1993. The last good game, at least for a long time. And the last good year, it seemed for a while—a marriage, a subsequent one, that appeared to be in pretty good shape; parents who were old but, for the last time, were healthy and enjoying life; a daughter, now a sophomore at Carolina, who had overcome her father's obsession and had become a basketball fan in her own right, a fervent floor-rusher after home victories over Duke; and a Democrat in the White House for the first time in twelve years. And the Heels were back on top. It was not that they had ever really been down in that decade since the 1982 championship. During that period they had ended the regular season ranked number one two or three times, had passed Kentucky as the all-time winningest college basketball program (a distinction the Wildcats have since reclaimed), had turned out a string of All-Americans, had made the Sweet Sixteen every year, and the Elite Eight several times. But they had reached the Final Four—their old accustomed place the last weekend in March—only once in the past decade, done in by injuries and upsets and bad luck, and that was unimaginable. But in '93 they were all the way back, ranked number one, with only Michigan's Fab Five standing in the way of another national title.

On the night itself, very cold for early April, we—my wife, her fourteen-year-old daughter, and I—went through the rituals in preparation for the Big One, building a fire, fielding good-luck calls from various parts of the country, positioning chairs for maximum positive effect, listening to the pregame spin. (My daughter was at some bar down on Franklin Street, ready to charge the barricades in the event of victory.) My wife had had a good year herself—she was a ferocious Bama football fan, and the Crimson Tide had won *them*selves a national title back in early January. And her daughter, a precocious sort who knew the game, was into both Tar Heel basketball and Tide football. I was feeling uncharacteristically social for such a big game, actually seeing it with other people, prancing and stalking during timeouts but otherwise controlling myself. And, of course, it came out the right way. Donald Williams went five for seven from three-point range for the second straight game, Chris Webber called his infamous time out (the equivalent of Fred Brown's errant pass to Worthy in '82), and Dean Smith had his second national title. We drove down to Franklin Street, joined fifty thousand people in celebrating, and all seemed right with the world.

Carolina-Kentucky, March 25, 1995. Much that had seemed right two years before had now gone wrong. Six months after that '93 championship, my mother had undergone unsuccessful heart surgery and, after struggling in the hospital for another five months, had died. My father, whose health had been good to that point, fell apart after that, and now himself was dying. Spending much of the past two years looking after parents hadn't done my marriage any good — Bama and I had been good together in the good times but not so good in the hard times — and it was almost over. About to split, we now occupied separate floors of the house, and I had retreated to my quarters that winter to find some solace in Tar Heel games. I hadn't yet gotten into my habit of taping games and seeing them later — mainly because I hadn't yet mastered the art of taping *anything* — so I had to see and absorb it all live. But it had been a good year for the Heels, 27–5, led by All-Americans Jerry Stackhouse and Rasheed Wallace, and most of the season the team had been in the nation's top five. Now, in the Southeast Regional finals, they were taking on the Kentucky Wildcats, most people's favorite to win the national title.

The Carolina-Kentucky rivalry was a longstanding one. Not that they went head-to-head that often, but they had dueled back and forth for several years for the distinction of having the most all-time college wins. The Heels were leading in that category coming into this game, and also held a 15–6 record against Kentucky in their limited head-to-head competition, but the Wildcats had won more national titles. Each school considered itself the top all-time program in college basketball, although in truth UCLA probably staked a better claim than either to that title.

Kentucky was favored in this particular game, and I was reconciled to a loss. Early that Saturday afternoon I turned on my upstairs TV, absorbed the pregame commentary—"The Wildcats are much deeper than the Tar Heels"—and saw the Heels get off to a bad start. Rasheed Wallace found himself in early foul trouble and had to go to the bench. Sensing defeat, I marshaled my defenses: we weren't supposed to win; it didn't matter that much anyway; of what value is basketball compared to the rest of my life? Then Wallace returned in the second half, Stackhouse had a sensational last twenty minutes, and the Heels won going away, 74–61, for another Final Four trip. As the last seconds ticked off, I was jumping and screaming, though no one was listening, save perhaps my Bama-fan wife in some remote part of the house. My mother was dead, my father dying, my marriage was over, but here I was yelling crazily over a basketball victory.

Carolina-Arizona, March 29, 1997. Off to the beach again to see a Final Four game, never a good thing to do. With a woman, Barbara, who was great in all other respects but seemed to bring bad luck for hoop. The year before, when I first met her, I had been with her at a conference, in a sports bar, when the Heels had taken a big lead over Arkansas in the national semifinals, then had seen some

Razorback hit a shot from past midcourt at the first-half buzzer to change the momentum and doom the Heels. And now, in the semifinals again, Arizona loomed—and Barbara was from Arizona, although she was a Sun Devil, not a Wildcat, and in this game she professed to be for the Heels. Still, her home state, a bad sign. It was a beautiful Saturday afternoon on the Outer Banks and, fearing what lay ahead, I was tempted to skip the game altogether, to call someone back in Chapel Hill to tape it for me and suggest that we head out to the beach. Why suffer, why endure it? But Dean Smith had just broken the all-time record for wins by a collegiate coach, and I thought the refs might give him some calls and the Heels might win. It started great—All-Americans Vince Carter and Antawn Jamison were sensational—but then the Heels fell apart, couldn't hit, and lost by eight.

We had dinner that night at a terrific seafood place, but I couldn't enjoy it. I couldn't get the question out of my mind: why did Shammond Williams, usually deadly from outside and never known for choking, choose this afternoon to have his worst shooting game of the year? I went back and took a long walk on the beach. Two years earlier, my life had been awful—two of the three things, divorce and the death of a parent, that are supposed to drive you into deep depression had just taken place—but we beat Kentucky and I was exultant. Now my life was great, I was at the Outer Banks with a beautiful woman, I had just gotten an endowed chair and good reviews of a couple of recent books, my daughter was happy, had a good job, and was about to get married to a nice guy (who had the added advantage of knowing nothing at all about basketball). But the Heels had just lost in the Final Four and I was miserable. Was something wrong here?

The Arizona game was momentous for several reasons. It was to be Coach Smith's last—though no one knew that at the time and would not until the following October when he announced his retirement. It was also the second of four straight losses the Tar Heels would suffer in the semi-final round of the Final Four—to Arkansas earlier, to Utah in 1998, and to Florida in 2000. Making the Final Four seemed easy—Carolina led the nation in that category and still does—but once there they seemed jinxed. The Heels were favored in three of the four semi-final losses, and in each game the same thing had happened: their reliable outside shooter picked the worst time in the season to go cold.

On a more personal level, the Arkansas, Arizona, Utah, and Florida losses in the Final Four were disturbing for another reason. I saw, or was to see, all of them with Barbara, and we lost them all. Most of the other games— regional finals and so forth—we had not seen together and the Heels had won. Could we make it this way? That I should ask the question seemed absurd: she was young, blonde, smart as hell, and looked great. But after 2000, for three or four years, I began to find reasons not to watch really important playoff games with her. Let her, at spring break, take off to Dominica for diving; I would stay in cold North Carolina and suffer.

Those were some of the games, significant enough in the larger world of college hoops but especially fraught with emotional baggage for me. But I have not even come to the game that, year after year, in good times and bad, meant more to a Tar Heel than any other—that is, the annual bloodbath, or two or three of them, against the hated Blue Devils. I have mentioned Will Blythe's estimate, in his *Sports Illustrated* piece, that Carolina versus Duke in basketball is "doubtless the greatest rivalry in college athletics, perhaps in all of sports," a rivalry so heated that Blythe has a book forthcoming on the subject with the exquisite title, *To Hate Like This Is to Be Happy Forever.* Some might say the Yankees versus the Red Sox is a greater rivalry—in England they would say Manchester United versus Leeds United or Tottenham versus Arsenal—but on the college level, in America, Blythe is certainly right.

The two schools are eight miles apart and competitors in everything (even in the number of Rhodes Scholars: as of 2005, the Heels led by two with the Devils surging), but their excellence on the hardwood makes the basketball rivalry particularly significant. Almost every game they play has some bearing on who is number one in the country. In fact, according to Durham sportswriter Al Featherston, it has been more than fifty years since at least one of the two teams wasn't nationally ranked when they played, and they have met 134 times in that span. (The Heels won seventy-eight of those, Duke fifty-six.) Twenty-three times they have met when one or the other was nationally number one. They lead the nation in reaching the Final Four, the Heels sixteen times, the Devils fourteen; in fact, more than half of the Final Fours over the past half century have had either Duke or Carolina in them. The Heels have won four national titles (five, counting one before the NCAA held its tournament), the Devils three.

That's why the rivalry is of *national* significance, but it doesn't fully explain why it is so important to me. I touched on a little of it earlier: like a lot of North Carolinians, I come from a house divided—my mother's family Duke, my father's, Carolina—though in fact Carolina ruled in my own household. But it is more than that: it's that Duke-Carolina fed into my early vision of life as morality play, going far beyond the hardwood. Dean Smith in Chapel Hill, then Mike Krzyzewski in Durham, became legendary figures in North Carolina, larger than life. They are alike in many ways—both midwesterners, rather unimpressive physical specimens, easily caricatured (Smith with his midwestern twang and outsized nose, Krzyzewski with his rodent-like features), who reached the top of their game through intelligence, hard work, iron discipline, and the undying devotion and loyalty of their players. But they are different too.

Unlike Coach K (as he is generally known in these Anglo-Saxon parts, Polish names seeming a little hard to pronounce and even harder to spell), who feels comfortable in the spotlight and loves appearing in high-profile ads for American Express and other companies, Smith generally has shunned the spotlight. I honestly believe he would have been just as happy as a high school teacher and coach back in Kansas, as his father had been. He truly hates the glitz, the commercialization of college basketball. When he coached he hated showboating (so does Coach K for that matter); I even got the feeling at times that Coach Smith disliked *scoring*. Defense and assists and boxing out and setting picks were what the game was about; it was as if scoring were self-indulgence, too much pleasure, a violation of Puritan austerity. Coach Smith was not, as has often been claimed, the only man to hold Michael Jordan under twenty points a game—in fact, Jordan as a sophomore averaged twenty on the dot—but in stressing defense and teamwork he did turn Jordan into basketball's Renaissance Man.

As I was about to say about Duke and Carolina as morality play, Smith and Krzyzewski have long played their roles, front and center, in that drama. But it began long before them, began with the nature of the two schools. Carolina is a public institution, the oldest state university in the country, annually rated one of the nation's four or five best, but still it is *public;* it has always been, in the words of alumnus Charles Kuralt, "the university of the people." Duke is private, *moneyed* (not that solidly endowed Carolina is poor), for much of its history a Methodist denominational institution but in recent years a southern extension of the Ivy League. Carolina has always been known as the liberal school, Duke, at least by comparison, the conservative one. The contrast was seen most starkly in the bitter 1950 North Carolina Senate race that had meant so much to my father. Willis Smith, the conservative lawyer and staunch segregationist, was chairman of the Duke board of trustees; Frank Porter Graham, the South's leading liberal and my father's old history teacher, was president of the University of North Carolina.

That was 1950, and Duke's brand of conservatism has changed since then—its faculty, in fact, is probably about as liberal as Carolina's. But not its basketball coach. Dean Smith has always been known as an outspoken liberal Democrat, taking bold stands on race, the death penalty, and the nuclear freeze, among many other issues. Krzyzewski is just as strong a conservative. Smith, who openly supports Democratic candidates, held a fund-raiser for recent Democratic senatorial candidate (and UNC alumnus) Erskine Bowles, the son of a prominent Tar Heel whose name graces the street running in front of the Dean Dome. (Bowles himself, after his Senate defeat, became president of the University of North Carolina.) Smith's longtime assistant and successor, Bill Guthridge, held another fund-raiser for the local liberal Democratic congressman. Krzyzewski, on the other hand, held a fund-raiser on the Duke campus for Bowles's 2002 Republican opponent, Duke graduate Elizabeth Dole. The curious admixture of politics and basketball hit the national stage in 2004 when (as Will Blythe recounts in his *Sports Illustrated* piece) Carolina law school alum—and, later, faculty member—John Edwards, campaigning for the Democratic nomination for president in Oregon, told a reporter that he "hates Duke basketball."

Most kids growing up in North Carolina—in fact, most diehard Devils and Heels fans anywhere and of whatever vintage—have no idea of the politics of the rivalry. They know only of the *games*, and there have been too many classics over the years to describe them in any detail: the 1974 game at Carolina when the Heels came from eight points down in the final seventeen seconds (in the days before three-point shots) to beat the Devils; the double-overtime battle at Duke in 1995, won by the

Heels 102–100; or several other overtime classics won by both Duke and Carolina, always followed (if the home team won) by jubilant fans rushing the court.

But the game that told me most about the Duke-Carolina rivalry and my own feelings about it did not involve Carolina at all, at least not on the court. It was the Duke-Connecticut national championship game in March 1999. Duke came in ranked number one, and was heavily favored to win the title. Unlike virtually all other Tar Heel fans, I was for them. I had *always* been for Duke when they played a nonconference team, especially in the NCAA tournament. The family connection. My own graduate degree from Duke. The school from my home state, after all, taking on whatever team from the Pacific Slope or Great Plains or Deep North they should happen to meet in the tournament.

So I went into Duke-UConn in 1999 being for the Blue Devils, and I think I was for them throughout the game. I was glad that the Huskies kept it close — it might be an exciting ending, after all — but I assumed that in crunch time I would go for the Devils. When that time came — the last minute, UConn up one, Duke with the ball — I wavered. I'd never faced this before, the last minute of a game and not knowing who I wanted to win. When Duke was called for traveling and forced to foul UConn with less than ten seconds to play, my thoughts went something like this: Carolina has three national titles (four, counting the 1924 one), Duke two. If they win, they will — by the conventional count — tie us. They're catching us in everything else; they're beating us more than we're beating them these days. I was for them as long as they were almost but not quite as good as we were. Noblesse oblige. But now they've gotten uppity; they're better than we are.

As Khalid El-Amin stepped to the line, I was no longer wavering. I realized I was for UConn—which is to say, I was against Duke. It wasn't Carolina playing in this game, but still it was, which is what every other Heel or Devil fan had always felt when the other was playing. But not, until now, me. But when El-Amin hit his two free throws and Duke's Trajan Langdon, trying to get off a game-tying three-pointer, dribbled into traffic and lost the ball—and the seconds ticked off to a UConn win—I jumped up and screamed as if the Heels had won the title. On the one hand, I was petty and mean-spirited. On the other, I had had an epiphany, a conversion. My grandfather, "one of the swiftest" halfbacks in Duke's early days, and my record-setting Duke cross-country uncle, would turn over in their graves, but I couldn't help it. I had seen the light.

March-April 2005. The Duke loss to Connecticut in 1999 only delayed the inevitable: the Devils came back to win the whole thing in 2001, tying the Heels in all-time NCAA titles. Even worse, it was bruited about basketball circles in the early years of the new century that Duke was now the premier program in college basketball—hard words to accept for Tar Heels who had once themselves been number one. After their Final Four appearance in 2000 the Heels entered their Slough of Despond. They were sliding even before that. Coach Smith had retired, and although his successor, Bill Guthridge, went to two Final Fours in three years, he was doing it largely with Coach Smith's recruits, and the pipeline was running dry. It was during this period—when the Heels could no longer be counted on to win close games, when even maintaining their national record twenty-win season streak was becoming a burden—that I began to tape their games and see them later.

I remember one moment in particular that captures the desperation of that immediate post–Dean Smith period: it was in the second round of the NCAAs in 2000 and the Heels (who had had such a bad year they were seeded eighth) had to beat number one seed and heavily favored Stanford in the Southeast regionals to win their twentieth game for the unheard-of thirtieth straight year. That (and beating Clemson at home every year for a half century) was about all we had left, other than cheering against Duke at the summit. But I saw no way to beat Stanford. I was in New York over spring break, visiting my daughter and her husband, and I could have stayed over Sunday afternoon to see the game with them. But I couldn't take this defeat, the ending of the last of many streaks tying the Heels to basketball glory.

So I called ahead to North Carolina to have the game taped, and went on a long walk with Jane and Graham during what would have been the first half, then packed up and left from northern Long Island, heading through Queens and Brooklyn and Staten Island into New Jersey. As I hit Brooklyn I knew I had to take the chance. I flipped on the dial, homed in on the station I knew would be carrying the game, and tried to determine from the play-by-play man's voice and the crowd noise what was happening, who was leading, how tight it was. After ten or fifteen seconds, not getting a score, I couldn't take it. I flipped it off, and then, about ten minutes later, now on Staten Island, turned it on again. The score came quickly this time: the Heels were leading by four with less than a minute to go.

I cut the radio off again and stared straight ahead, across the bridge into New Jersey, and made my deal with the basketball gods: If you will only give me this one—just let the twenty-win season streak continue one more year—I won't ask for anything else. I don't care if they lose the next one; I don't care if it ends next season; that will be thirty in a row, and no one will ever touch that. Just don't let it end here. The game was almost certainly over by now, but it took me a full ten minutes to turn the radio back on, and there was the Heels' Ed Cota talking. A good sign: they probably wouldn't be interviewing him if we'd lost. We *had* won, 60–53. I threw my hands up and banged the roof, driving with my knees, as a driver a couple of lanes over looked at me like I was crazy.

That's how far we had fallen, cheering a twenty-victory season that that been a given in Tar Heel country for three decades. And, of course, it got worse. After one more winning season, this one under new coach Matt Doherty—in which the Heels defied expectations by beating Duke at Duke, winning eighteen in a row and rising to number one in the country—they fell apart completely. In 2001–2002 they suffered through the worst season in a century of Carolina basketball, and the next year wasn't much better. Sportswriters everywhere dragged out the parallels with Greek tragedy, the pride and then the fall. The Heels, pundits said, had forgotten how to win. By 2003–2004 they had a new coach, Roy Williams, a native Tar Heel who'd had great success at Kansas, and they had plenty of young talent, but they still couldn't win the close ones—a trademark of Carolina basketball forever. My external-events index reached an all-time low between 2001 and 2004: the Heels were abysmal on the gridiron, not much better on the hard-wood, and the GOP controlled the White House and al-most all else.

Others had high hopes for 2004–2005, however, and I too got my season tickets for the Dean Dome, though for away games I still wasn't ready to give up my tape-delays and emotional loss insurance. Or, even worse, in early season, I *was* ready to give them up. I didn't think I cared that much any more. The 2004 presidential race had taken all the competitive fire out of me, had left me bro-ken and defeated. If anything athletic at all appealed to me through December and early January, it was football: it seemed so much more sensible, as well as more aesthet-ically pleasing, than basketball. That, of course, had hap-pened to me before, through bowl season, but this time it lasted into early February, about the time of the first Duke game, at Cameron.

For the first time all year I taped a game: although the Heels had lost only twice all season and were slightly fa-vored over the Devils, I had forebodings. So I retreated to the bedroom and watched a PBS documentary, letting Barbara take over the den, then trading places with her when she appeared at the door, signaling the game was over. I fell into old habits, rewinding the tape without checking the score, then replaying it chunk by chunk until I came to the last eighteen seconds — Duke up by one, Carolina's ball. It was the fourth straight game against Duke that had come down to the last possession, and we had lost them all. Out of the timeout Raymond Felton took the ball, was open for a jumper but didn't take it (*why* didn't he take it?), instead dribbled toward the right corner, lost the ball and lost the game. I played it again, running the tape back and forth, and nothing changed. Why hadn't he taken the open shot? I had two lectures to prepare for the next day, but I stayed up until 2 a.m. pondering that question. I cared fervently again. I was back.

I wasn't all the way back, though, until the second Duke game, the final game of the regular season, at the Dean Dome. I knew I was back when I dreamed the night before of the Devils' J. J. Redick and Bill Melchionni draining NBA-range three-pointers, something they had done with regularity all season. The Heels were the better team, number one in the ACC, number two in the country, but they had lost four in a row to Duke, and besides it was senior day, which meant two or three walk-ons would start and the Heels, as always on senior day, would fall behind. It was also Barbara's first live Carolina-Duke game, and she had her game face on as much as I did, glaring at the ticket-taker who blithely remarked, "Enjoy the game."

I can't say we enjoyed it, but we endured it, and we won, and then we enjoyed what came after. In fact, Duke did start hot; with Redick hitting everything in sight in the first half and Melchionni in the second, the game appeared out of reach with 2:45 left and the Devils up by nine. At that point the Heels put on a rally worthy of the Dean Smith era, cutting the lead to one with twenty seconds left and going in front on a three-point play by freshman Marvin Williams a couple of seconds later. But most games that come down to the last possession really come down to *two* last possessions, and Duke had its chance. They set a pick for Redick, he came off it clean and wide open and, just as in the dream, shot with perfect form—and missed. The ball bounded out to another Devil who shot and missed, and the game was over. I'd been in plenty of Carolina celebrations before, but this one was different; a sort of desperation was involved, and a great release, a catharsis at the end. And for me, personally, another sort of relief: after all the Final Four losses, we'd finally won a big one with Barbara looking on.

The real season—what aficionados call the second season—was still to come. Basketball, as ESPN sages constantly remind us, is a tournament sport, and that's where championships are decided. But some tournaments mean more than others. The Heels lost in the second round of the ACC tourney, and that didn't bother me greatly—although Duke beat Georgia Tech for the title, tying the Blue Devils with Carolina for the record number of ACC titles, and that did bother me. (Again, no matter who either is playing, it's always, on some level, Carolina versus Duke.) In fact, history has shown that losing in the ACC tournament usually helps a top-notch team, usually either Duke or Carolina, in the bigger tournament to come.

Filling out my 2005 NCAA brackets with my customary fan's caution, I picked the Heels to go out in the second round. (In recent years I have sometimes won my department pool that way; and if I am wrong, I am happy.) Others, pundits and amateurs, saw for them a loftier destiny: the near consensus—I gathered from watching three hours of ESPN analysis on Brackets Sunday—was that the number two Heels were on their way to the finals to meet top-ranked Illinois. That sounded reasonable, but in fact one versus two rarely happens—had not happened, in fact, in thirty years.

The first two rounds provided plenty of drama for others but little for the Tar Heels. The third-round game against Villanova, with Felton on the bench with foul trouble during crucial stretches, was much closer. In fact, Carolina was lucky to survive. The game against Wisconsin in the regional finals, which turned out to be almost as close, presented me with a particular challenge: how to have 2 p.m. Easter dinner with my daughter and son-in-law, now back in North Carolina, and still see the Carolina game which was on at the same time—or, if I taped it, how to keep others (for there were to be other guests) from seeing it live. Negotiations ensued and my daughter issued her ruling: a television would be available upstairs for anyone who wanted to see it but under no circumstances was anyone to let her crazy father know the score. One of the other guests, Jane's mother and my former wife—no doubt recalling from thirty years before my manner of watching a televised game—approved of the solution.

I had surveyed the Heels' progress in the early rounds with one eye on Duke, had watched while Ferret Face—as Barbara had come to call Krzyzewski—tied, then broke,

Dean Smith's all-time record for NCAA tournament wins. (But that isn't fair, I protested to anyone who would listen; teams plays more tournament games now.) NCAA tournament spectatorship is always a dual challenge, playing both offense and defense, wanting your team to win and, if you're honest with yourself, wanting certain other teams to lose. Duke obliged in the third round, just after the record-breaking win, being taken out by Michigan State. After the Spartans, frequent Final Four residents themselves, beat Kentucky in the regional finals, they were set to meet Carolina the next weekend in the national semifinals.

When I turned on the TV the next Saturday afternoon for the three-hour pregame show, basketball was not on. The Pope had died only an hour before. My first reaction — admit it, basketball fans, yours would be too — was at least mild concern that the Pope's death, coming just as Final Four Saturday was getting under way, might preempt television coverage. Then I felt ashamed of such sentiments and thought I should be considering the larger consequences of his death. Then one possible consequence did occur to me. My thinking went something like this: Michigan State is coached by Tom Izzo, and Tom Izzo, I think, is Catholic. The Spartans also probably have more Catholics on their roster than the Tar Heels. Will that inspire them? Bobby Knight won, remember, the day Reagan was shot — quite literally, won one for the Gipper. Would Izzo — I wondered briefly before banishing such heresy — win one for the Pope?

In fact, for all I know, Izzo isn't Catholic at all, but I went over the range of possibilities for a full three hours.

Could it be that the basketball Heels don't do well when the outside world impinges on their game? Smith did lose to Knight in 1981 after all. And I recall, in January 1977, a Tar Heel midseason slump in late January just after *Roots* was televised. For some reason—something he had said in an interview or something I imagined—I had actually wondered if Phil Ford had been affected by the series. What made me think that an African American player at Carolina might have been more affected than an African American player at, say, Maryland or Kentucky or Marquette? Put it down as an index of the seriously disturbed mind of a basketball fan that I actually, if mildly, entertained the thought at the time.

But this was 2005, and I was more rational now, and Izzo didn't win. I saw the game from beginning to end, never flinching, though jerking and twisting on occasion. I had vowed to watch all Final Four games live, none of this taping, and on Monday night, against Illinois for the national championship, I stuck with it. Monday had been the sort of memorable day all national championship days are when your team is playing that night: just as I recall almost everything (or think I do) about March 23, 1957, when I was thirteen and the Heels won their first title, I remember the day of almost all other Tar Heel title games, and certainly one so recent as April 2005. Spring had come to Chapel Hill, it was very warm, and the ubiquitous Bradford pear trees were in bloom. I remember what I taught that day: Ralph Ellison's *Invisible Man*. I remember who came by during office hours. I recall seeing students walk across campus, more even than usual on their cell phones, and remember thinking if an invader came from outer space he would think that these contraptions pressed against the sides of their heads had something to do with the way these human beings moved, the way they were propelled across campus.

If you've come this far, you know the outcome of the game that night. The Tar Heels defeated their third Big Ten team in as many games and won the NCAA championship, 75–70, in the first title game in three decades between the nation's consensus two best teams. Sean May, whose father had led Indiana to the 1976 national title, led the 2005 Heels to theirs. You can't say the Illinois game wiped out all the painful memories of 2001–2004, but it helped. When freshman Marvin Williams, who had hit the game winner against Duke a month before, hit the game winner against the Illini—and Raymond Felton intercepted a pass and hit his free throws to seal the win—it was over. There are no original ways to respond in times like these: you jump up, hit the ceiling, grab anyone near for a bear hug and, if you're in Chapel Hill, take off for Franklin Street.

It should end there, right? My team, which three years ago was among the nation's worst, was now the nation's best. I was there in downtown Chapel Hill, as I had been in 1993, with fifty thousand people, even a number of them my own age, shouting and singing and jumping over bonfires. Next year, I remember thinking, could be even better: three All-Americans are juniors, another potential All-American is a freshman, and Roy Williams, the Tar Heel coach who came home from Kansas to win his first national title, is one of the best.

But, of course, it couldn't end that way. The next day

Rashad McCants, the enigmatic star labeled "Mystery Man" on *Sports Illustrated*'s preseason basketball cover, announced he was leaving school and turning pro. A few weeks later May and Felton and Marvin Williams said the same thing. Who could blame them? Their stock was sky high, and they had given us what we wanted. And that should be enough. Fans of the Illini or the Deacs or any number of other basketball powers would sell their souls for *one* national title. I had four, five if you count the Tar Heel way, and I wanted more. That's always the way it is: even Bruins' fans, when UCLA had its remarkable run in the 1960s and '70s, always wanted more.

So I focus on next year, and what do I see: a team that could have been among the nation's best ever, with *four* projected top twelve draft choices, instead will be without 92 percent of its offense. The leading returning scorer, I consider, averaged 3.9 for the season, and one returning player scored—one point—in the championship game. I look next door at Duke and see that *nobody* is going pro early (well, nobody that counts anyway), that nearly everybody will be coming back, that the Devils have already been named next season's number one. I should be rejoicing over the championship but what do I do: I look into next season and see the abyss.

Coda

So here I am, in late middle age, with my faded and tattered Carolina practice jersey still hanging in an upstairs closet, a washed-up athlete with a bum knee, an aching back, and bone spurs at the base of each thumb — all in all, the relics of a once passable mammal. Here I am, as a fan, in the aftermath of a glorious championship, retreating again into a sort of grim stoicism, inured to defeat at the hands of a coalition of Blue Devils and Republicans. I take stock: not really a very good player, at least on the college level, and, in recent years, a generally wretched fan.

Are the two linked, I ask myself, the player and the fan? If I had been better at the first, would I have been happier as the other? If I'd had an all-around game good enough to land me on the varsity for three years — where I would have practiced two hours a day almost every day from October through March for three years and taken so many road trips I would have tired of them — would I have gotten it out of my system? If I'd wanted it more then, would I want it so much now? And, since that wasn't the case, has all this time watching and reading and thinking about basketball since then been a waste of time? Has it been worth it after all?

For one moment at least it was, one late summer night in 1996 when I was meeting my daughter at the airport. Waiting in the terminal, I saw Dean Smith for the first time (other than from my lofty perch in the Dean Dome) in five or six years. He'd been on a flight arriving, I think, from Pittsburgh, but given the lateness of the hour and his celebrity in our state, the attendants had apparently let him off first so he could escape the throng that would follow shortly. First, I wondered what he had been doing in Pittsburgh. What McDonald's All-American loomed in those precincts? Then I decided it wouldn't slow him down too much if I hailed him for a minute.

He was gracious, unrushed, as always, remembering my name and asking how the teaching and writing were going. (From two or three previous encounters, I recalled he was a little uncertain whether it was literature or history or philosophy I taught—something in the humanities, he always knew that.) Then he asked if I was still playing any basketball. I pointed to my left leg, with the zipper scar running up it, and said, well, a little tennis, but no more basketball.

"That's too bad," he said. "You were one of the best jumpers we ever had."

I knew it wasn't true, of course, and he knew it wasn't true, and my usual instinct in a situation like that would be to bring things back to reality—to qualify, to modify, to deflect, to deny altogether. One of the best jumpers we ever had. Sure. Along with Worthy, Jordan, Stackhouse,

Carter. But on this occasion I didn't touch it, didn't respond at all, just let the words stand, and went on to some other pleasantry such as wishing him a good upcoming season, and he was gone.

After he left I stood there wondering why he had said that. Well, first, I realized, it demonstrated his legendary memory. After nearly thirty-five years he did recall the one thing I could do well. No Carolina-class leaper was I, as Carolina leaping came to be defined in and after the Age of Jordan, but I could dunk and he remembered that. Second, could he have meant "one of the best jumpers" among our walk-ons? Yes, that was possible. Also, could there have been, subconsciously, a racial subtext: one of the best *white* jumpers we ever had? No, not that: there had been Cunningham and Bob Lewis and Larry Miller, and, besides, Dean Smith was one of the most color-blind coaches ever. That left only one thing: Dean Smith was not only on course to become the winningest coach in college basketball history (a goal he reached seven months later) but he was also, as I already knew, a very kind and generous man.

"One of the best jumpers we ever had." Not even close.

But it sure had a nice ring to it.

Acknowledgments

My greatest debts are to Beverly Jarrett, director of the University of Missouri Press, and Bruce Clayton, series editor, not only for encouraging me to do this book but also, once it was under way, keeping after me until it was done. They convinced me that, for a time at least, I should put away such pursuits as American literature and southern intellectual history and keep my eye on the prize—basketball. I am also grateful for the assistance of others at the Press, particularly John Brenner, Beth Chandler, Jennifer Cropp, Jane Lago, and Karen Renner.

Others—family, friends, and colleagues—also helped in numerous ways: my sisters, Jane Hobson and Alice Hobson Dudley, who helped me pin down early memories; Bryan Giemza, fact-checker extraordinaire (when you ask whether a mourning dove "coos," he tells you exactly when and where and in what key it coos); my daughter, Jane, and son-in-law Graham for assistance of various kinds; for information and advice, Nicolas Allen, Chris Armitage, Will Blythe, Bill Boring, Art Casciato, Jim Coleman, David Davis, Elliott Gorn, Bill Harmon, Bill Henderson, Linda Whitney Hobson, Hunter James, Andy Matthews, Lucinda MacKethan, Bob McMahon,

Diane Roberts, Greg Robinson, Jim Seay, Myron Tuman, Ralph Voss, Nina Wallace, and Jim Williams; and, finally, Barbara Bennett, who shared much of the last chapter of this book with me, provided invaluable editorial advice in its writing, and survived hoop season only because she too came to see basketball as a matter of transcendent importance.

About the Author

Fred Hobson is Lineberger Professor of Humanities at the University of North Carolina at Chapel Hill. He is the author of numerous books, including *The Silencing of Emily Mullen and Other Essays* and *Tell about the South: The Southern Rage to Explain.*